Weniger Fehler in der Klassenarbeit

Englisch

Grammatik 5|6

Schroedel

Weniger Fehler in der Klassenarbeit

Englisch Grammatik 5|6

Autor:
Bernd Raczkowsky unterrichtet Englisch an einem Gymnasium und ist seit mehr als 30 Jahren im Schuldienst tätig. Seine bisherigen Tätigkeitsbereiche umfassen unter anderem die Fachbetreuung Englisch, die Leitung studienbegleitender Seminare in Kooperation mit der Universität Augsburg, die Mitarbeit in der Schulleitung und die Koordination verschiedenartiger fremdsprachlicher und allgemeinpädagogischer Aktivitäten und Programme.

Druck [1] / Jahr 2016

Redaktion: imprint, Zusmarshausen
Kontakt: lernhilfen@schroedel.de
Umschlaggestaltung: Janssen Kahlert Design & Kommunikation GmbH, Hannover
Umschlagfoto: Duc John Nguyen
Innenlayout: tiff.any GmbH, Berlin
Illustrationen: Thies Schwarz, Hannover
Druck und Bindung: westermann druck GmbH, Braunschweig

ISBN 978-3-507-**23093**-4

Inhaltsverzeichnis

Vorwort

Liebe Schülerin, lieber Schüler,

du möchtest weniger Fehler machen und deine Noten verbessern?
Dann ist **Weniger Fehler in der Klassenarbeit** genau das Richtige für dich!
Weniger Fehler in der Klassenarbeit hilft dir, typische Fehler zu vermeiden und so deine Leistungen zu steigern.

Zu jedem wichtigen Thema gibt es ein Kapitel. Jedes Kapitel beginnt mit einem Auszug aus einer Klassenarbeit. Hier siehst du, welche Fehler häufig gemacht werden. Sind in deiner Klassenarbeit ähnliche Fehler angestrichen? Dann solltest du dieses Kapitel auf jeden Fall bearbeiten!

Die Kapitel bestehen aus folgenden Bausteinen:

Regeln	Hier wird leicht verständlich erklärt, welche Regeln du beachten musst, um typische Fehler zu vermeiden.
Übungen	Mithilfe der Übungen kannst du die Regeln aktiv trainieren.
Tipps	Eingestreute Tipps geben dir zusätzliche Hilfestellungen.
Fehler-Check	Am Ende des Kapitels kannst du den Test machen: Alles fehlerfrei?

Die **Lösungen** zu den Übungen und zum Fehler-Check findest du am Ende des Buches.

Und nun kannst du dem Fehlerteufel den Kampf ansagen!

Viel Erfolg wünscht dir
Bernd Raczkowsky

Grundlegende Fehler – leicht vermeidbar!

Fehlerquelle Pronomen

Hello, me name's Percy. I'm one of the magic forest dwarfs. We're live //
under the root of an old spruce together with my parents.
These say they're can't afford a better place to live, because new //
apartments in the woods are too expensive. So there dream of a /
bigger house hasn't come true. I don't blame they for their economic /
way of life. It's simply is they're money. Curly, my brother, left our two ///
months ago to start his apprenticeship* as a magician at he's aunt's /
'School for Future Witches and Magic Dwarfs'**.

*apprenticeship = Lehre/Ausbildung; **dwarf = Zwerg

Regeln

Pronomen sind wesentliche Bestandteile von Sätzen. Bei ihrer Verwendung musst du zunächst die beiden folgenden Gruppen unterscheiden:

1. Personalpronomen im **Subjektfall**

Singular			Plural		
1. Person	2. Person	3. Person	1. Person	2. Person	3. Person
I	***you***	***he/she/it***	***we***	***you***	***they***
ich	du	er/sie/es	wir	ihr	sie

Achtung: ***I*** wird immer groß geschrieben, egal an welcher Position im Satz.

Beispiele: *I speak English. Do you live in Birmingham? Is he tired? She likes jazz music. It sometimes rains in August. We must leave now. Do you know lasagne? They know how to behave.*

2. Personalpronomen im **Objektfall**

Singular			Plural		
1. Person	2. Person	3. Person	1. Person	2. Person	3. Person
me	***you***	***him/her/ it***	***us***	***you***	***them***
mir/mich	dir/dich	ihm/ihn ihr/sie ihm/es	uns/uns	euch/ euch	ihnen/sie

Bei den deutschen Bezeichnungen stellt die Form vor dem Schrägstrich die Dativform (Frage: wem oder was?) dar, jene dahinter die Akkusativform (Frage: wen oder was?).
Damit wird schnell klar: Im Englischen unterscheidet man bei den Objektpronomen nicht zwischen Dativ und Akkusativ.
Das macht das Lernen der Formen natürlich viel einfacher!

Übungen

1 Übersetze die folgenden Kurzsätze ins Englische.

a) Kannst du mich hören?

____

b) Kannst du mir helfen?

____

c) Ich liebe dich.

____

d) Ich glaube dir.

____

e) Du triffst ihn oft.

____

f) Erzähle ihm die Geschichte.

____

g) Mag er sie? (das Mädchen)

____

h) Vertraue ihr.

____

i) Sie besuchen uns oft.

____

j) Sie geben uns Geld.

____

k) Ich brauche euch.

____

l) Er schreibt euch bald.

____

2 Setze die richtigen Pronomen im Subjektfall bzw. im Objektfall ein.

a) "Can _______ hear _______, Lucy?"

"Yes, _______ can, but I can't see _______."

b) Mike is fourteen, _______'s not twelve.

His sister's twelve and _______'s as bold as brass.

c) Don't touch _______, Susan. He's in a bad mood.

d) We don't know how to solve this problem.

So can _______ please give _______ some advice.

e) Don't tell _______ lies, my son.

I know that _______ always try to find excuses.

f) Come on, give _______ a new chance.

They have never disappointed _______ so far.

3 Verbessere die Fehler im Klassenarbeitsauszug auf Seite 5. Schreibe in dein Heft.

Tipp Aufgepasst! Die folgenden Formen lassen sich leicht miteinander verwechseln. Präge dir die Unterschiede gut ein.

he's	Kurzform von *he is* (er ist)
his	‚besitzanzeigend' 3. Person Singular männl. (sein)
it's	Kurzform von *it is* (es ist)
its	‚besitzanzeigend' 3. P. Sing. sächlich (sein)
you're	Kurzform von *you are* (du bist/ihr seid)
your	‚besitzanzeigend' 2. P. Sing./Plural (dein(e), euer(e))
they're	Kurzform von *they are* (sie sind)
there	dort, da
their	‚besitzanzeigend' 3. P. Plural (ihr(e))

Fehler-Check

Setze die richtigen Pronomen ein.

1. Mary, why don't ______ want to come to ______ birthday party? All my friends except (*außer*) you will be there!
2. You must call ______ this afternoon. I need some advice (*Rat*).
3. Have ______ seen my new bike, Gilbert? Isn't ______ wonderful?
4. Why doesn't your sister like me, Daisy? I like ______.
5. One day, when Oliver and ______ friends came home, they saw ______, a beauty, a princess!
6. Thomas A. Edison was born in ______ grandfather's house in 1847.
7. You must see the Millers, Hannah. Please meet ______ at Trafalgar Square.
8. I don't like those people. ______ don't really see my problem.
9. ______'re really kind, Mr Benson. But can you help ______ one more time?
10. Sssh – the kids are sleeping. ______ had a hard day.
11. Why don't ______ call the police, Victor? They can help ______.
12. Excuse me, can you please show ______ the way to the station?
13. Go to Marta's father. He is a dentist. And ______'s a good one.
14. I know, ______ don't believe me, Jo. But ______'m telling the truth.

Punkte	16–20 Punkte	15–10 Punkte	weniger als 10 Punkte
	Sehr gut!	Akzeptabel!	Übe noch einmal!

He, she, it – das „-*s*" muss mit!

Rebecca <u>work</u> at Sullivan's Media, a CD shop, in her summer holidays /
for six hours a week. Does she <u>likes</u> her job? Yesterday her father /
<u>askeds</u> her about her customers, but she didn't <u>answers</u> his questions. //
She now just <u>want</u> to relax* because her work at Sullivan's is so hard. /

*relax = sich entspannen

Regel

Im ***simple present*** muss bei der **dritten Person Singular** (also bei *he, she* und *it*) grundsätzlich ein **-s** an das Verb angehängt werden.
Beispiel: *My uncle lives in Southampton.*

Übung

1 Hinter jedem Verb des folgenden Textes befindet sich eine kleine Lücke. Entscheide, wo du ein -s einsetzen musst.

Tom collect ___ posters. He like ___ pop posters best. Pop posters, he think ___, are the most wonderful of all posters. Whenever there is a pop concert in his town, he want ___ to get ___ one of the posters fixed to the boards in the streets. Sometimes he ask ___ for a poster at the tourist office and he can usually have ___ one. Very often, his friends, who know ___ that he is interested in pop posters, give ___ him a nice new poster as a birthday present. His father know ___ about his son's hobby, so when his colleagues' children go ___ to a pop event, he always say ___: "Don't forget ___ to look ___ for posters!"

Regeln

Beachte die folgenden **Sonderformen**:

1. Endet die Grundform eines Verbs auf **-*y* nach Konsonant**, dann wird dieses -*y* zu -*i* und es wird -es angehängt (also **-*ies***).
   Beispiel: *carry → He carries his sister's suitcase.*
   Dies gilt nicht, wenn die Grundform des Verbs auf -y nach Vokal endet.
   Beispiel: *buy → He buys a lot of books every month.*

2. Endet die Grundform eines Verbs auf einen Zischlaut (z. B. ***-s, -ch*** oder ***-sh***), dann wird ***-es*** (statt -s) angehängt.
   Beispiele:
   catch → He always catches a lot of fish in this part of the river.
   brush → She brushes her teeth twice a day.
   kiss → He sometimes kisses his girlfriend.

3. Besonderheiten: Die dritte Person Singular von *go* und *do* endet im *simple present* ebenfalls auf ***-es***:
   Beispiele: *She often goes to the cinema. He never does the dishes.*

Tipp | Wenn du dir nicht sicher bist, ob das Verb auf einen Zischlaut endet, dann mache ganz einfach die „Zungenbrecherprobe“: Hänge gedanklich ein -s an und überprüfe, ob das Verb dann noch gut aussprechbar ist oder ob es eigenartig klingt. Das wäre z. B. bei folgenden Beispielen der Fall: *He ~~washs~~ ...; Mary ~~kisss~~ ...; My brother ~~fetchs~~ ...*

Übung

2 Setze die richtigen Endungen ein: -s, -*es* oder -*ies*

a) Susan never go ______ to school by bus, she walk ______.

b) My younger sister often cr ______ (cry) when she's alone at home.

c) Max often switch ______ on the lights in his room in the afternoon.

d) Her daughter usually do ______ her homework in the kitchen.

e) He pay ___ a lot for his mobile phone calls every month.

f) Fred attend ___ a language course abroad, so he miss ___ his family.

Regel

Nach **modalen Hilfsverben** *(modal auxiliaries)*, wie etwa *can, may, must, can't, mustn't, needn't, could, might* usw., wird in der 3. Person Singular Präsens weder an das Hilfsverb noch an das Vollverb ein -s angehängt!

Beispiele:

RIGHT: *She mustn't ask me so many questions. It might rain.*
He must always be home by eight o' clock in the evening.
WRONG: *She ~~musts~~ learn a lot for her A-level. Terry can ~~speaks~~ Spanish.*
Aunt Lou ~~coulds gives~~ us a lift to the train station.

Übung

3 Bilde aus den Bruchstücken richtige bejahte Aussagesätze.

a) **Ken ▪ might ▪ know ▪ much more ▪ about ▪ the secret**

b) **Charlotte ▪ spend ▪ in Scotland ▪ want to ▪ her summer holiday**

c) **sister ▪ his ▪ her homework ▪ do ▪ must ▪ in her room**

d) **she ▪ go ▪ never ▪ on Sundays ▪ to church**

Regel

In den meisten **Fragesätzen** und **verneinten Aussagesätzen** werden in der 3. Person Singular Präsens die Formen ***does*** bzw. ***doesn't*** verwendet. Das zu *does* oder *doesn't* gehörende Vollverb erhält dann kein angehängtes -s.

Beispiele:

Does her English teacher know about her problems at home?
Sven *doesn't like dogs very much, to be honest, he hates them.*

Tipp | Du kannst dir die letztgenannte Regel ganz einfach merken: In *does* und *doesn't* steht bereits ein s, deshalb brauchst du keines mehr beim Vollverb!

Übungen

4 *Mediation:* Setze die folgenden Sprechsituationen ins Englische um.

a) Du fragst, ob Sally's Bruder in New York City lebt.

____

b) Du teilst jemandem mit, dass dein Vater seine Freunde nicht zu seiner Geburtstagsparty einlädt.

____

____

c) Du fragst, ob dieser Schrank wirklich in das Schlafzimmer deiner Eltern passt. (passen = *fit*)

____

____

____

____

____

5 Der folgende Text enthält zahlreiche Fehler, die bereits unterstrichen wurden. Verbessere sie in der rechten Spalte.

My strange English teacher

My English teacher is a strange person. He look likes a dog, but he don't like animals. He know much about the Chinese language, but he can't speaks English. He often gos out in the evening but he never talk to young ladies. Every week he buies hundreds of postcards at the stationer's*, but he never pay for them. He wants to gets married, but he doesn't likes families. He dream bad dreams every night, so he must cries a lot. He can't sees very well, but he don't wear his glasses. He musts work a lot, but he doesn't goes on holiday. He always feel sick, but he never see the doctor. He often rushs to school but his never late. He can't carries his heavy bag but he doesn't wants to buy a car. He don't smile although he tell us many jokes. He doesn't talks much in his lessons but he never finish them in time. Everyone know that he's just so strange!

*stationer = Zeitschriften-/Schreibwarenhändler

Fehler-Check

Übertrage die Verben der rechten Spalte ins Englische und setze deren richtige Form in die Lücken ein.

Pete's big problem	
Once a year in summer Pete ________________	reisen müssen
to his aunt in New York City. He __________	lieben
America, but he ________________ going on a	nicht mögen
plane. Although so many planes ________ across	fliegen
the Atlantic Ocean every day, he ______________	nicht verstehen
____ why only few people ______________ flying.	Angst haben vor
When asked for the reason for this, he __________	nicht können
give a good answer. He often ________ to the	gehen
airport and ____________ the jets, but he	beobachten
__________ the idea of being on one of them.	hassen
________ he __________ how safe flying on	wissen
a plane really is? At least it ____________ to	scheinen
be safer than going by car. His uncle, who ________	arbeiten
as a pilot, always ________: "The most dangerous	sagen
part of an air travel is the lift to the airport in a	
taxi!" He ______________ giving this statement.	gerne mögen

☐ Punkte	**12–15 Punkte** Klasse!	**7–11 Punkte** Okay!	**weniger als 7 Punkte** Noch einmal üben!

Word order – Ordnung im Satz

Steven walks to school never in winter. When it's too cold, he takes //
always the bus into town. Then he arrives at 8.15 at school. But this /
morning he must be early there, because his friend Tom wants to him //
meet at 8.00 in front of the gym to discuss a big problem – how to
learn maths within two days to pass on Friday their test. /

Regeln

In englischen Aussagesätzen (bejaht und verneint) und in den meisten englischen Fragesätzen lautet die Reihenfolge, in der die einzelnen Satzteile zusammengefügt werden müssen, folgendermaßen:

1. Im einfachen Satz: S – V – O *(subject – verb – object)*
   Beispiel: *He (= S) earns (= V) a lot of money (= O).*

2. Im Satz mit Orts- und Zeitangabe:
   S – V – O – P – T *(subject – verb – object – place – time)*
   Beispiel: *He (= S) meets (= V) his friends (= O) in Munich (= P) every Tuesday (= T).*

Tipp | Stelle dir einfach das Wort SPORT vor. Statt V *(verb)* steht hier die genauere Bezeichnung Prädikat P *(predicate)*. Während eines Fußballspiels kickt jemand das ‚Bein' des R weg. Übrig bleibt also SPOPT – die Reihenfolge der Satzteile im englischen Satz.

Übung

1 Ordne die folgenden Bruchstücke und bilde Sätze mit richtiger Satzordnung.

a) **in Brooklyn ▪ she ▪ last Wednesday ▪ him ▪ saw**	
b) **Sue ▪ on the playground ▪ heard ▪ yesterday ▪ a strange noise**	
c) **did not answer ▪ that day ▪ David ▪ that question**	
d) **take ▪ many pictures ▪ you ▪ last week ▪ at your party ▪ did ▪ ?**	

Regeln

1. Enthält ein Satz ein **direktes** (wen oder was?) und ein **indirektes Objekt** (wem oder was?), so gilt:
   indirektes Objekt vor direktem Objekt
   Beispiel: *She gave him the book.* → $S – P – O_{indirekt} – O_{direkt}$

2. Enthält ein Satz ein **Adverb der Häufigkeit** (*adverb of frequency*), so steht dieses **vor dem Verb**. Somit ergibt sich folgende Reihenfolge:
   $S – Adv_{Häufigkeit} – V – O – P – T$
   Beispiel: *He often visited his aunt in Los Angeles this summer.*

Übungen

2 Übersetze die folgenden deutschen Sätze ins Englische.

a) Hast du mir das Geld gestern wirklich gegeben?

____

b) Ich habe ihm das Buch zurückgeschickt, aber er hat es nie erhalten.

c) Mr Benson lehrt mich Latein.

d) Hast du ihm viele Briefe geschrieben?

e) Darf ich dir einen Witz erzählen?

3 Platziere das Adverb der Häufigkeit an der richtigen Stelle.
Beispiel: *She trusts* her friends. (usually)*
→ She usually trusts her friends.

a) Tom writes letters. (never)

b) My mum takes the bus to Soho. (sometimes)

c) He's seen a ghost in his room. (often)

d) My aunt has been a gossip** girl. (always)

*to trust = vertrauen; **gossip = Gerede/Tratsch/Geschwätz

Fehler-Check

***Mediation.* Übertrage die folgenden Sprechsituationen ins Englische.**
(Für die richtige Reihenfolge der Wörter erhältst du pro Satz einen Punkt.)

1. Teile deinem Vater mit, dass du ihm gerne eine Frage stellen willst.

   ____

2. Erzähle Alan, dass du seine Freundin letzte Woche in Bath getroffen hast. ______________________________

3. Frage Isabella, ob sie wirklich jeden Tag in Greenwich Tennis spielt.

   ____

4. Sage, dass du nachmittags oft in der Schule bleibst.

   ____

5. Bitte den Kellner, dir eine Tasse Tee zu bringen. Could ______________________________

   ____

6. Teile mit, dass du den Nebel in San Francisco nicht magst.

   ____

7. Frage Priscilla, wie viele Bücher sie ihrem Bruder an Weihnachten bereits geschenkt (gegeben) hat. ______________________________

   ____

8. Fordere Pete auf, dir die Wahrheit zu sagen.

   ____

☐ Punkte	7–8 Punkte	4–6 Punkte	weniger als 4 Punkte
	Astrein!	In Ordnung!	Übe noch einmal!

There is ..., there are ..., this, that, these, those

Portsmouth is a nice place to spend a couple of days in summer. It gives many old ships there. You can have a guided tour on the HMS Victory, a three-mast sailing ship. These ship once was Britain's pride. There's a lot of old buildings in the harbour quarter and there're many shops to buy souvenirs. That town is really magnificent both for tourists and inhabitants.

Regeln

There is ... und ***There are ...*** sind wichtige Formulierungshilfen, um das deutsche *Es gibt* ... (seltener: *Da ist* ..., *Da sind* ...) im Englischen auszudrücken. *There is* ... wird für den Singular, *There are* ... für den Plural verwendet. Im Singular gibt es auch die verkürzte Form *There's* ...

Beispiele: *There is/There's much work to do.*
There are too many mistakes in your dictation, Pete.
Is there any question? Are there many tourists?

Übungen

1 Setze die folgenden Sprechabsichten ins Englische um.

a) Frage nach, ob es in Australien viele deutsche Einwanderer (= *immigrants*) gibt.

____

____

b) Frage Lily, ob auf ihrem Bankkonto (= *bank account*) viel Geld ist (ob es dort viel Geld gibt). ______________________________

____

c) Klage darüber, dass es in Schottland so viel Regen gibt.

____

d) Teile mit, dass da im Bus 20 Schüler sitzen (sind).

____

2 Im Zoo. Bilde Aussagesätze. Beginne mit *There is* ... bzw. *There are* ...

Regeln

This und ***that*** sind sogenannte Demonstrativpronomen.

1. ***This*** bedeutet „dieser/diese/dieses“. Die dazu gehörende Mehrzahlform lautet ***these***. *This* und *these* werden für Dinge oder Personen verwendet, die sich in der Nähe des Sprechenden befinden.
2. ***That*** bedeutet „jener/jene/jenes“. Die dazu gehörende Mehrzahlform lautet ***those***. *That* und *those* werden verwendet, wenn man auf etwas weiter weg Liegendes hinweisen will.

*Look at **this** tree!*

*Look at **that** tree!*

Tipp Häufig findest du bei *this* und *these* die zusätzliche Ortsangabe *here*, bei *that* und *those* die Ortsangabe (*over*) *there* (da drüben).
Beispiele: *Can you see that pencil-case over there?*
These holes here were dug by rabbits, but those holes over there were made by mice.

Übung

3 Du bist Zeuge eines Autounfalls. Berichte auf Englisch, was du gesehen hast. Schreibe in dein Heft.

Du hast gesehen, dass ...

a) ... dieses Fahrrad hier von rechts kam.
b) ... jenes grüne Auto da drüben nicht angehalten hat.
c) ... jene zwei Jogger dort drüben den Unfall nicht sehen konnten (= *couldn’t*).
d) ... diese Reifenspuren (= *wheel traces*) hier von einem anderen Auto sind.
e) ... diese Frau hier alles sah.

Fehler-Check

Setze ein: *there is, there are, this, that, these, those, here, (over) there*

Good morning, ___________ is Julia Sullivan reporting from ___________ year's tennis cup final in Southampton. ___________ already hundreds of spectators sitting on _________ upper seats over ___________ opposite to me. They are waiting for the players to come and start ___________ important match. ___________ n't much time left, so the match will start in a couple of minutes. ___________ a strange murmur in the stadium because you can see ___________ dark, grey clouds approaching from the west. Will ___________ match be started, or must all people find shelter from the rain in one of ___________ shelter huts over ___________?
Oh, my God, what's ___________? ___________ a first thunderbolt! Look, all ___________ people over there are running down to the entrance gates. They don't want to be struck by lightning, they want to leave ______ terrible scene! And it's becoming foggy. I can see _____________ monitor in front of me, but I can't see ___________ people in the next row not far away. What a disaster! And right now it starts raining.
I don't like ___________ weather. ________________ so many people, and they all want to go home now. ___________ nowhere to stay because all ___________ people are nervously pacing around.

☐ **Punkte**	**18–22 Punkte** Einwandfrei!	**11–17 Punkte** In Ordnung!	**weniger als 11 Punkte** Arbeite nach!

s-Genitiv oder *of*-Genitiv?

Listen. Of course, I'm my fathers son. His two sister's daughters are //
Anne and Susan. They're not my parents kids but my aunt's children. //
So, they're my nieces. The friends of my nieces often play tennis with /
me. One of them is called Dennis. Dennis strong point in tennis is his /
terrible forehand.

Regeln

1. Um den **Genitiv** richtig zu bilden, musst du dir erst einmal folgende Frage stellen: Ist das Bezugswort, (zu) dem etwas gehört oder auf das sich etwas bezieht, eine Person oder nicht?
   Wenn es sich um eine Person handelt, verwendest du den **s-Genitiv**. Wenn nicht, verwendest du den ***of*-Genitiv**.
   Beispiele:
   Pete's new bike is blue. (s-Genitiv, Bezugswort Peter ist eine Person)
   The roof of this house is new. (*of*-Genitiv, Bezugswort *this house* ist keine Person)
2. So bildest du den **s-Genitiv im Singular**:
   Personelles Bezugswort im Singular + Apostroph (') + s
   Beispiele: *my sister's diary; William's kite; our neighbour's dog*
3. So bildest du den **s-Genitiv im Plural**:
   Personelles Bezugswort im Plural + Apostroph (')
   Beispiele: *her parents' car; the Millers' garage*
4. So bildest du den ***of*-Genitiv (Singular und Plural)**:
   Beispiele: *the University of Columbia; the sons and daughters of this nation; the beauty of these beaches; the colour of her eyes*

5. Den Genitiv der unregelmäßigen Pluralformen ***people*** (Leute, Menschen) und ***children*** bildest du folgendermaßen:
unregelmäßiges Pluralwort + Apostroph (') + s
Beispiele: *those people's tickets; our children's interests*

Übungen

1 Welche Genitiv-Formen sind richtig, welche falsch? Kreuze an.

	Genitiv-Formen	richtig	falsch
a)	*... her uncles' wife ...*	☐	☐
b)	*... the ground floor of this building ...*	☐	☐
c)	*... the suitcases of my sister ...*	☐	☐
d)	*... Tom's computer ...*	☐	☐
e)	*... our children's comic books ...*	☐	☐
f)	*... the Thomsons' bedroom ...*	☐	☐
g)	*... Donald Ducks' nephews ...*	☐	☐
h)	*... the walls of this room ...*	☐	☐
i)	*... Lydias' dream ...*	☐	☐
j)	*... Mr and Mrs Johnson's new home ...*	☐	☐
k)	*... this street's name ...*	☐	☐

Tipp Einige Sonderfälle beim Genitivgebrauch musst du dir ganz einfach merken und als Ganzes lernen:
- Sie ist beim (geht zum) Arzt. → *She's **at (goes to) the doctor's**.*
- Sie ist bei Victoria zu Hause. → *She's **at Victoria's**.*
- bei den Millers zu Hause → ***at the Millers'***
- in der Apotheke → ***at the chemist's***

2 Übersetze ins Englische. Schreibe in dein Heft.

a) das Buch meines Bruders
b) der Titel dieser Geschichte
c) das Problem der Familie Miller
d) die Fragen der Kinder
e) die Bäume im Garten der Clarks
f) Freds Geheimnis
g) die Fahrräder dieser Leute
h) die Farbe dieser Blume

3 Bilde die richtigen Genitiv-Formen.

 my nephew  his two dogs	a) I like ______________________. ______________________
 our parents  new house	b) Our ______________________. ______________________ is quite big.
title 	c) I know ______________________ ______________________
 these people  clothes	d) These ______________________ ______________________ wet.

Tipp

Was machst du bei Personen, deren Namen auf einen Zischlaut enden (z. B. -s oder -*sh*)?
In einem solchen Fall musst du folgende Regeln beachten:

Singular	Plural
Agnes → Agnes's ball	Mr and Mrs Dash → the Dashs' bikes
Louis → Louis's schoolbag	oder: → the Dashes' bikes

4 Streiche die falschen Alternativen durch.

a) The Irvings'/Irving's/Irvings model railway was rather expensive.
b) I don't like the colours in Cathys/Cathies/Cathy's new room.
c) The Cavendishs/Cavendish's/Cavendishes' garage is painted blue.
d) Dennis/Dennis's kindergarten class is called 'The Rugby Fighters'.

Fehler-Check

Fülle die Lücken mit den richtigen Genitiv-Formen.

Hi, Steven,

You want to know something about ______________________ (my brother, stay) in New York City? Here you are. ______________________________ (name, school) is Southpark High. Some months ago __________________ (my parents, plan) was to fly over to New York to see if everything's alright. I'm sure they wanted to see ____________________________________ (the host family, home) and the ______________________________ (surroundings, this interesting city). In a letter, however, my brother wrote about __________________ (his friends, plans) of taking him along on a trip to Chicago. To be honest, I think it was _________________________ (my brother, idea) to keep my parents away with this letter. He doesn't want to have them with him in New York because he's got a girlfriend there, called Paris. __________________ (Paris, parents) live in ________________________________ (most expensive borough*, New York). ____________________ (her relatives, homes) are in ___________ ______________ (the heart, Manhattan). I must end now, because I have to go to _________________ (doctor). I sprained** _______________ __________________(ankle, left foot) in a basketball match yesterday.

☐ Punkte	**11–13 Punkte**	**6–10 Punkte**	**weniger als 6 Punkte**
	Grandios!	In Ordnung!	Übe noch einmal!

*borough = Stadtviertel/Stadtteil (amerikanisch) ; **to sprain = verstauchen

Articles – bestimmt oder unbestimmt?

Once there was the house with many mice in it. A old cat that also //
lived in the house caught mice one by one and ate them. The mice /
were so afraid that they decided to hide in their holes and ask an /
unicorn for a help. "That's too bad. I must get them out by an trick", //
said the cat to herself. She climbed up the wall and let herself hang /
down. So a cat pretended to be dead. A mice saw the cat hanging //
there. ...

Regeln

1. Im Englischen erscheint die Verwendung des Artikels recht einfach, denn du musst nicht wie im Deutschen zwischen den Geschlechtern (der, die, das, ein, eine, ein) unterscheiden.
   Der **bestimmte Artikel** lautet im Englischen immer ***the*** (der, die, das).
   Beispiele: *the ball; the stairs; the Browns; the black shirt; the orange*

2. Der **unbestimmte Artikel** lautet meist ***a*** (ein, eine, ein). Es gibt eine Ausnahme: Statt *a* wird ***an*** verwendet, wenn das darauffolgende Wort mit einem Selbstlaut beginnt.
   Beispiele: *a ball; a horse; a tree;*
   aber: *an orange ball; an apple; an ugly wallpaper*

Tipp Du kannst dir die Sache mit dem Selbstlaut ganz einfach mit dem Wort *another* (noch ein, noch eine) merken, allerdings mit dem Unterschied, dass dieses Wort zusammengeschrieben wird, der Artikel aber niemals an das folgende Wort ‚angedockt' wird.

Übungen

1 Übersetze die folgenden Artikel-Adjektiv-Nomen-Gruppen ins Englische.

a) ein teurer Bleistift ______________________________

b) die wunderbaren Strände ______________________________

c) eine fantastische Aussicht ______________________________

d) ein alter Bär ______________________________

e) das beste Hotel ______________________________

2 Setze, wenn nötig, *a* oder *an* ein.

I'm packing my bags, because I'm going to fly to Venice soon. In my big suitcase I've got _____ green shirt, _____ extra pair of shoes, _____ woolen coat, _____ orange braces, _____ pair of brown trousers, _____ old-fashioned hat, _____ grey slippers and _____ old teddy bear.

Tipp Vorsicht! Man schreibt *an ugly face* (ein hässliches Gesicht), aber *a unique song* (ein einzigartiges Lied), denn *ugly* beginnt mit einem Selbstlaut, *unique* hingegen mit einem j-Laut (Lautschrift: [ju:ni:k]).

3 Setze *a* oder *an* ein.

a) _____ universal truth

b) _____ olive scarf

c) _____ United Airlines flight

d) _____ audiovisual show

e) _____ Indian meal

f) _____ university

g) _____ angry man

h) _____ idea

Regeln

Abstrakte Nomen bezeichnen etwas, das nicht gegenständlich fassbar ist. Der bestimmte Artikel wird bei abstrakten Nomen folgendermaßen verwendet:

a) Werden diese Nomen auf etwas **Allgemeines** bezogen, wird kein bestimmter Artikel gesetzt.
Beispiele: *Do you like music? She loves life.*

b) Werden diese Nomen jedoch näher bestimmt und auf etwas **Spezielles** bezogen, wird ***the*** gesetzt.
Beispiele: *Do you like the music of the 70s? She loves the life in L.A.*

Übung

4 Der Regisseur Franze Romanze möchte seine Filme auch in den USA verkaufen. Dazu muss er seine Filmtitel ins Englische übersetzen. Erledige du die Arbeit für ihn.

a) Schweigen (*silence*) ist golden ______________________________

b) Das Schweigen der Hämmer ______________________________

c) Das Leben des Herzens ______________________________

d) Stell' dich (*face*) dem Leben! ______________________________

e) Liebe kann heilen (*heal*) ______________________________

f) Die Liebe seines Lebens ______________________________

Tipp

In folgenden Fällen wird meist der bestimmte Artikel gesetzt:
- Fluss- und Meeresnamen: *the Mississippi, the Pacific Ocean*
- Spielen von Musikinstrumenten: *He plays the guitar/the flute.*
- geographische Namen im Plural: *the Alps, the West Indies*

Der bestimmte Artikel wird **nie** gesetzt bei:
- den meisten Straßennamen: *in Fleet Street, next to Key Road*
- Institutionen (allgemein): *at school, to go to church*
- Medien (allgemein): *on TV, watch TV, aber: on the radio*
- Mahlzeiten: *they have dinner/breakfast/lunch/coffee/tea*

Fehler-Check

Setze, wenn nötig, *the, a* oder *an* ein.

a) After ____ dinner, he went down to ____ discotheque in ____ Boston Road, where he met ____ beautiful girl – ____ very love of his life. ____ life was back!

b) Oh, good heavens, are you really ____ man I got married to in ____ Alps in ____ December?

c) ____ old lady told her she saw her play ____ violin years ago on ____ TV.

d) I like ____ literature in general, but I don't like ____ literature of the Nineties.

e) ____ orange shirts hung on ____ old rotten line in ____ Bond Street.

f) "I was always late for ____ lunch at ____ school", he said on ____ radio.

g) ____ Pacific Ocean is ____ biggest of all oceans.

h) ____ United Nations commission decided on the problem of poverty in ____ Africa.

i) ____ money is not too important in ____ life!

j) Are you really telling me that ____ money I gave you on ____ Monday is gone?

☐ Punkte	22–28 Punkte	14–21 Punkte	weniger als 14 Punkte
	Super!	In Ordnung!	Noch einmal bitte!

Have got oder *have*?

My friend Anatomus is an alien from a planet in the Andromeda system.
He hasn't two but three eyes. He have four tentacles and green //
skin. He doesn't have got any legs. He's two big wheels to move on //
and he got red long hair. Has he a nose? No, he's got two of them! //
Does he have got a face? Of course, he've got the most wonderful //
face in the universe and the best smile!

Regeln

Das deutsche Vollverb **haben** kann man im Englischen auf zweierlei Weise ausdrücken: entweder mit dem englischen Vollverb ***have*** oder mit der Form ***have got***.

Beispiel: *Ich habe zwei Schwestern.*

→ *I have two sisters.* (Vollverb *have*)

→ *I have got two sisters.* (*have got*)

Have got wird sehr häufig im britischen Englisch verwendet.
Im amerikanischen Englisch findet man meist das Vollverb ***have***.

Übung

1 Übersetze. Verwende dabei das Vollverb *have* oder *have got* (siehe Klammern). Tipp: Achte auf die richtigen Formen *(I have, he/she/it has ...)*!

a) Sie hat furchtbare Probleme. *(have)*

____

b) Ihr habt zehn Minuten (Zeit). *(have got)*

____

c) Die Millers haben drei Autos. *(have)*

____

d) Pete hat zwei Schwestern. *(have got)*

____

Tipp

Have got wird besonders in Aussagesätzen des gesprochenen Englisch oft in seiner Kurzform verwendet:
Singular: *I've got; you've got; he's got; she's got; it's got*
Plural: *we've got; you've got; they've got*
Vorsicht Verwechslungsgefahr:
She's a child. → Sie ist ein Kind. (*she's* = Kurzform von *she is*)
She's got a child. → Sie hat ein Kind. (*she's* = Kurzform von *she has*)

2 Setze verkürzte Formen von *have got* ein.

a) She ____________ two bikes and brandnew rollerskates.

b) My mother ____________ three sisters.

c) They ____________ so many books in their living-room.

d) I ____________ a big, big problem.

e) We ____________ a lot of uncles and aunts.

Regeln: Verneinungen und Fragen

1. *Have got* verneinst du mit *haven't got/hasn't got/hadn't got.*
Beispiel: *They have got a big house.* → *They <u>haven't got</u> a big house.*

2. Das Vollverb *have* verneinst du mithilfe von *don't/doesn't/didn't.*
Beispiel: *They have a big house.* → *They <u>don't have</u> a big house.*

3. Bei Fragen mit dem Vollverb *have* brauchst du ebenfalls eine Umschreibung mit *do, does, did* bzw. *don't/doesn't/didn't.*

deutsch	***have*** **(Vollverb)**	***have got***
Hast du eine Schwester?	*Do you have a sister?*	*Have you got a sister?*
Hat er keinen Schlüssel?	*Doesn't he have a key?*	*Hasn't he got a key?*
Hatte Sie ein Fahrrad?	*Did she have a bike?*	*Had she got a bike?*

4. Bei Fragen, auf die nur mit *nein* oder *ja* geantwortet wird *(yes-/no-questions)*, können folgende Kurzantworten verwendet werden:
   a) Bei Verwendung des Vollverbs *have*:
   Do you have a car? – Yes, I do./No, I don't.
   Does he have a problem? – Yes, he does./No, he doesn't.
   Did she have a new bike? – Yes, she did./No, she didn't.
   b) Bei Verwendung von *have got*:
   Have you got a car? – Yes, I have./No, I haven't.
   Has he got a problem? – Yes, he has./No, he hasn't.
   Had she got a new bike? – Yes, she had./No, she hadn't.

Übungen

3 Übersetze. Verwende *have* oder *have got*. Schreibe in dein Heft.

a) Hat er nicht zwei Schwestern? – Doch./Ja. *(have)*
b) Die Prestons haben keine neue Garage. *(have got)*
c) Hattest du keine Antwort auf diese Frage? *(have)*
d) Ich habe keine Ahnung *(idea)*. *(have)*
e) Ich habe keine Ahnung *(idea)*. *(have got)*
f) Haben sie ein neues Auto? – Ja. *(have)*
g) Hast du einen Bleistift? – Ja. *(have got)*
h) Sie hat zwei Pferde. *(have got)*

4 Verbessere den Klassenarbeitsauszug auf S. 31. Schreibe in dein Heft.

Fehler-Check

Setze die passenden Formen von *have* oder *have got* ein.

a) _____ Lynn got a nice room? – No, she ________ It's far too small.

b) _____ your parents _____ trouble with your younger sister? – Yes, they do. My sister _____ got a lot of problems at the moment.

c) Sue: I really _____ have too much time, so hurry up, please. Ann: _____ you got more time tomorrow? Sue: I'm afraid, I ________.

d) She __________ a brother, but she __________ got two more sisters.

e) Have you _____ some tools? – Tools? – Yes, I mean, _____ you have a hammer, a screwdriver and a knife? – Yes, I _____ .

f) _____ Mary got a headache? – No, she _______ .

g) My uncle _____ _____ a big family. _____ he have twins? – No, he ________. He' s _____ three girls, two boys and four dogs.

h) Does Sue _____ her exercise-books at home? – Yes, she _____ .

i) My aunt's _____ blue earrings.

j) I _____ 't _____ much pocket money a week. How much _____ you have?

k) Hey, _____ you have my pen? – No, I ________. I've _____ my own.

l) He _____ never _____ much time. He's always hurrying.

☐ Punkte	23–31 Punkte Hervorragend!	15–22 Punkte In Ordnung!	weniger als 15 Punkte Übe noch einmal!

False friends

Dear Olivia,

How <u>goes it you?</u> Imagine, I <u>became</u> my new notebook yesterday. //
I waited all day, and finally, late in the afternoon, my father handed
me over a <u>brief</u> from the headmaster of our school. It said that I had /
been <u>brave</u> in class, so there wasn't any <u>ground</u> for having an extra //
lesson every week. My father congratulated on this good news saying:
"I haven't got a new <u>handy</u> for you, but this notebook here will be yours, /
because I'm very happy you improved* at school." So my father's really
got a better <u>meaning</u> of me. /

*to improve = (ver)bessern

Regel

False friends (wörtlich: falsche Freunde) sind englische Wörter oder Wendungen, die deutschen Wörtern ähneln, aber eine ganz andere Bedeutung haben. Sie sind daher eine typische Fehlerquelle.

Beispiele:

Ich bekomme ein neues Buch.
FALSCH: *I ~~become~~ a new book.* (*become* = werden)
RICHTIG: *I get a new book.*

Wie geht es dir?
FALSCH: *~~How goes it you~~?*
RICHTIG: *How are you?*

Er ist ein stiller Junge.
FALSCH: *~~He's a still boy~~.* (*still* = noch)
RICHTIG: *He's a quiet boy.*

Typische *false friends*:

brav ≠ *brave* (mutig) → ***well-behaved***
Er ist ein braver Schüler. → *He's a well-behaved pupil.*

Brief ≠ *brief* (kurz) → ***letter***
Sie schrieb einen Brief. → *She wrote a letter.*

Gift ≠ *gift* (Geschenk) → ***poison***
das Gift der Klapperschlange → *the poison of the rattlesnake*

Grund ≠ *ground* ((Erd)Boden) → ***reason***
Was ist der Grund dafür? → *What's the reason for this?*

Handy ≠ *handy* (praktisch, nützlich) → ***mobile/cell phone***
Mein Handy fiel runter. → *My mobile fell down.*

Kaffee ≠ *café* (Café, Restaurant) → ***coffee***
Kann ich einen Kaffee bekommen? → *Can I have a cup of coffee?*

Marmelade ≠ *marmalade* (Zitrus-Marmelade) → ***jam***
Ich mag Marmelade gerne. → *I like jam very much.*

Meinung ≠ *meaning* (Bedeutung/Sinn) → ***opinion***
Meiner Meinung nach ist das einfach. → *In my opinion it's easy.*

Rat ≠ *rat* (Ratte) → ***advice***
Ich brauche deinen Rat. → *I need your advice.*

Rezept (Arzt) ≠ *receipt* (Quittung) → ***prescription***
Der Arzt gab mir ein Rezept. → *The doctor gave me a prescription.*

Rezept (kochen) ≠ *receipt* (Quittung) → ***recipe***
Dieses Nudelrezept ist toll! → *This noodle recipe is great!*

sensibel ≠ *sensible* (vernünftig) → ***sensitive***
Sie ist schüchtern und sensibel. → *She's shy and sensitive.*

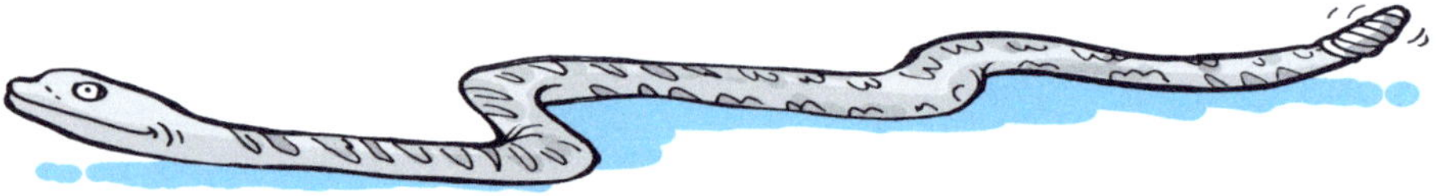

Übungen

1 Verbessere den Klassenarbeitsauszug auf S. 35. Schreibe in dein Heft.

2 Finde die Fehler in den folgenden Sätzen und verbessere sie.

a) Tim is a brave child, he never drinks his sister's café.

b) I think we should paint the bedroom yellow. What's your meaning?

c) My skin is very sensible.

d) We thought our dog had swallowed *(schlucken)* some gift. He was very still.

e) This strawberry marmalade is great!

f) She is a very sensitive and still person.

g) My father's rat is often handy.

3 Übersetze die folgenden Sätze.

a) Eine mutige, aber sensible Ratte wollte die Ferien in einem stillen Café verbringen.

b) Ein braver Junge schrieb einen Brief über ein Nudelrezept.

Fehler-Check

Setze die fehlenden Wörter ein.

a) Dr Hudson gave me a __________ *(Rezept)* against my terrible headache. He was of the __________ *(Meinung)* that I have caught a heavy cold.

b) This __________ *(Rezept)* is from my grandma.

c) He has bought nice __________ *(Geschenke)* for all his family.

d) What would you like for breakfast? – I would like to have a cup of __________ *(Kaffee)*, bread and butter and some orange __________ *(Marmelade)*.

e) Oh, the battery's run down. Can I please use your __________ *(Handy)* to call my mum? – Yes, you can, but you're __________ *(noch)* on time to get home.

f) Did you __________ *(bekommen)* a new skateboard? – Yes, I did. My father gave me a blue one some days before he __________ *(wurde)* the headmaster of Lincoln School.

g) May I give you some __________ *(Rat)*? Take an umbrella. It's going to rain.

h) Excuse me, the __________ *(Grund)* why I am late is: I couldn't find my __________ *(Handy)*.

☐ **Punkte**	**11–13 Punkte** Hervorragend!	**6–10 Punkte** In Ordnung!	**weniger als 6 Punkte** Übe noch einmal!

Fehlerquellen rund ums Nomen

Plurals – regelmäßig oder unregelmäßig?

Last night Katie had a terrible dream. She was on a small plane to
London about 10.000 <u>feets</u> high together with two <u>mens</u>. Two //
young <u>childs</u> were on the plane, too. All the <u>peoples</u> looked //
down and saw <u>sheeps</u> and <u>gooses</u> on the ground. Then the //
pilot started to land. But on the runway they all saw <u>hundred</u> /
of <u>mouses</u> and a lot of <u>woman</u> sitting on big yellow <u>cushion</u>. ///
“Katie, get up! It's time for school!“, her mother suddenly shouted.
What a pity. Oh no, now she didn't know how the pilot saved all the
<u>passengers</u> <u>lifes</u>! //

Regeln

Im Englischen werden die meisten Nomen **auf regelmäßige Weise** in den Plural (die Mehrzahl) gesetzt. Das geschieht einfach durch **Anhängen von -s** an die Singularform (Einzahlform).
Beispiele: *table → tables; kid → kids; girl → girls; boy → boys; teacher → teachers; lion → lions; window → windows; friend → friends*

Auf einige **Besonderheiten** bei der regelmäßigen Pluralbildung musst du aber achten:

1. Endet der Singular auf **-*y* nach Konsonant** (Mitlaut), dann wird im Plural aus dem **-*y*** ein **-*ies***.
   Beispiele: *country → countries; study → studies*
   aber: *boy → boys; way → ways* (da im Singular -*y* nach Vokal!)

2. Endet das Nomen im Singular auf einen **Zischlaut**, so wird im Plural **-*es*** angehängt.
   Beispiele: *kiss → kisses; patch → patches; church → churches*

Übungen

1 Was ist auf den Bildern zu sehen? Bilde die richtigen Pluralformen.

four trees

____

____

____

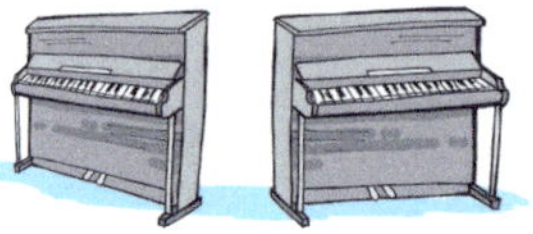

____

____

2 Bilde die richtigen Pluralformen. Achte auf Sonderfälle!

a) I know all the ______________ in the world. (country)

b) He ate half a kilo of ______________. (cherry)

c) Are the ______________ still at school? (kid)

d) She must prepare for the test within five ____________. (day)

e) My two ______________ are on holiday at the moment. (boss)

f) Our house has got twelve ______________. (window)

g) This is one of the most beautiful __________ in England. (bay)

h) Do you know these red ____________ over there? (berry)

i) There are so many ____________ in Scotland. (river)

j) Oh, look at these beautiful ____________ . (watch)

Regeln

Zwei weitere Gruppen besonderer Pluralformen solltest du dir merken.

1. Da sind zum einen die **unregelmäßige Pluralformen**:

deutsch	Singular	Plural
Mann/Männer	*man*	*men*
Frau/Frauen	*woman*	*women*
Fuß/Füße	*foot*	*feet*
Zahn/Zähne	*tooth*	*teeth*
Maus/Mäuse	*mouse*	*mice*
Kind/Kinder	*child*	*children*
Gans/Gänse	*goose*	*geese*
Ochse/Ochsen	*ox*	*oxen*
Schaf/Schafe	*sheep*	*sheep*

2. Nomen, die im Singular auf ***-f*** oder ***-fe*** enden, enden im Plural meist auf ***-ves***:
Beispiele: *shelf → shelves; wife → wives; knife → knives; calf → calves*

Tipp | *People* ist bereits eine Pluralform, bekommt deshalb kein **-s** und bedeutet „die Menschen“, „die Leute“. Beachte den folgenden Genitiv: *People's opinions …* → die Meinungen der Leute.

Übung

3 Setze die richtigen Pluralformen ein.

On this photo I can see three ________ (Gänse), five ___________ (Frauen), two ___________ (Kinder), four ___________ (Regale), a ________ (Schaf), six ___________ (Männer), nine __________ (Ochsen), eight _________ (Messer), two _________ (Mäuse), ten ___________ (Zähne), three ___________ (Kälber) and two ___________ (Füße).

Fehler-Check

Finde die falschen Pluralformen und korrigiere sie in der Spalte rechts.

a) I got ten kisss on my cheek from my little cousin Edward. ___________
b) Mr Spearmint, the dentist, said: "Your toothes are okay." ___________
c) Look, the lorrys are being loaded with tons of sand. ___________
d) Last night I dreamt of three mens and two womens. They had really big foots. They were talking to their four childs and playing with six gooses and two sheep. ___________ ___________ ___________
e) He doesn't want to watch the finals on TV. He likes being in the stadium to see the matchs live. ___________ ___________
f) The boies and girls were quietly sitting on their chaires. ___________
g) She knows the capitals of most countrys. ___________
h) Please put the books on the shelfs. ___________
i) On his voyage Paul sailed into four different baies. ___________
j) Four eys can see more than only two. ___________
k) Don't forget to brush your teeths. ___________
l) Our childs' new dog is called Alexander the Great. ___________
m) So many peoples have died in the plane crash. ___________

☐ Punkte	15–18 Punkte	9–14 Punkte	weniger als 9 Punkte
	Hervorragend!	In Ordnung!	Übe noch einmal!

Mengenangaben: *some* oder *any, much* oder *many?*

Lemon and potato cake

Heat 225 grams butter in a cake tin. Cream the butter and a //
half kilo sugar in a bowl. Whisk in any potatoes. Crack in some /
eggs. Don't use too much of them. Mix half a kilo flour with one //
teaspoon baking powder and put it in the bowl with the sugar. /
Some further instructions cannot be given because I don't know /
how to finish the cake. Better ask any of your friends. /

Regeln: *some* oder *any?*

1. Die Mengenangabe ***some*** wird im Deutschen mit „einige" oder „etwas" wiedergegeben. *Some* wird in **bejahten Aussagesätzen** verwendet.
   Beispiele: *He bought some books.* (einige Bücher)
   He bought some sugar. (etwas Zucker)

2. In **verneinten Aussagesätzen** und in **Fragesätzen** wird dagegen ***any*** verwendet.
   Beispiele: *There aren't any books on the shelf.* (Da sind keine Bücher im Regal.)
   Are there any books on the shelf? (Sind da Bücher im Regal?)

Übung

1 Setze *some* oder *any* ein.

a) I'm sorry, there isn't _______ coffee left. You must take _______ tea.

b) He had _______ quick answers, but they didn't make _______ sense.

c) Teacher: Are there _______ questions? No? Then let's do _______ work.

d) Sophie hasn't got _______ money left.

Tipp Du kannst *some* auch in Fragen verwenden, wenn du mit diesen Fragen um etwas bittest oder etwas anbietest.
Beispiele: *Can I have some jam, please? Would you like to have some eggs?*

Regel: *no*

Du kannst statt *not any* auch *no* (kein, keine, keines) verwenden.
No findet sich im gesprochenen Englisch öfter als im geschriebenen.
Beispiel: *There is no time left.* Statt: *There isn't any time left.*

Übung

2 Übertrage die folgenden Sprechabsichten ins Englische. Schreibe in dein Heft.

a) Teile jemandem mit, dass es für dieses Verhalten *(behaviour)* keine Entschuldigung *(excuse)* gibt. (Verwende *no*.)
b) Teile jemandem mit, dass es für dieses Verhalten keine Entschuldigung gibt. (Verwende *any*.)
c) Frage, ob du etwas Käse haben kannst.
d) Frage, ob (überhaupt) Käse da ist.
e) Sage, dass du einige der Jungen aus Boston kennst.
f) Teile mit, dass du keinen der Jungen aus Boston kennst.
g) Biete Leah etwas Marmelade an. (Beginne mit: *Would you like ...*)
h) Sage, dass du keine Ahnung *(idea)* hast. (Verwende *no*.)
i) Sage, dass du keine Ahnung hast. (Verwende *any*.)

Regeln: *much* oder *many*?

1. ***Much*** bedeutet „viel". Es wird bei Nomen verwendet, die man nicht zählen kann, wie z.B. *snow* (~~one snow~~, ~~two snows~~, ~~three snows~~).
Beispiele: *There's much work to do. I haven't got much time.*

2. ***Many*** bedeutet „viele". Es wird bei zählbaren Nomen verwendet.
Beispiele: *I saw many birds on the rock. She's got many friends.*

Übung

3 Übersetze. Verwende dabei *much* oder *many*.

viel Spaß ____________________	viele Menschen ____________________
viel Geld ____________________	viele Tiere ____________________
viele Wörter ____________________	viel Liebe ____________________
viel Sand ____________________	viele Lineale ____________________

Tipp | *A lot of* („viel, viele") kann bei zählbaren **und** nicht zählbaren Nomen verwendet werden: *a lot of birds; a lot of work; a lot of money.*

Regel: Mengenangaben mit *of*

Of ist ein sehr wichtiges Wörtchen, um Mengen anzugeben. Im Gegensatz zum Deutschen, wo man z.B. sagt, „eine Flasche Wasser", „zwei Kilo Mehl", muss im Englischen *of* eingefügt werden: *a bottle of water, two kilos of flour.*

Übungen

4 Übersetze den Einkaufszettel. Schreibe in dein Heft.

4 Orangen
2 Flaschen Milch
1 Kilo Butter
2 Tafeln *(bars)* Schokolade
1 Liter Apfelsaft
4 Packungen Reis

5 Verbessere den Klassenarbeitsauszug auf S. 43. Schreibe in dein Heft.

Fehler-Check

In den folgenden Sätzen sind mehrere Mengenangaben enthalten, von denen aber nur jeweils eine richtig ist. Kreise die richtige Lösung ein.

a) Don't eat too many/much/any chocolate.

b) Have you got much/any/no idea how to translate this sentence?

c) A lot of/Any/Much people think ice-hockey is a brutal sport.

d) How much/any/many/a lot of roads must a man walk down ...

e) I'd like to have a cup --/of/some tea, please.

f) There's much/any/no way out!

g) Can I have some/any mustard, please?

h) This really doesn't make many/a lot of/no/any sense.

i) Steven hasn't got a lot of/much/no/any pets. He's only got a rabbit.

j) There's too many/any/a lot of/much water in the pot.

k) In my pencil-case I've got many/much pencils and much/some rulers.

l) I don't understand. Can you please give me a lot of/some/no advice?

m) Any/No/Some dogs are really aggressive.

n) A sportscar is any/no/a lot of/much faster than a limousine.

o) Pooh, there isn't many/no/any salt in this soup. How awful!

p) I've been to much/no/many countries in Europe, but the country I like very many/any/some/much is Switzerland.

q) Can't you see that there is too many/some/much milk in the cup?

Punkte	15–19 Punkte	9–14 Punkte	weniger als 9 Punkte
	Hervorragend!	In Ordnung!	Übe noch einmal!

Zeitformen *(tenses)* richtig gebrauchen

3

Simple present oder *present progressive*?

An e-mail

"Hello, John. I <u>spend</u> my holiday here in Florence. /
The sun <u>shines</u> and a strong wind <u>blows</u> at the moment. I <u>sit</u> here ///
in one of the nice cafe´s. <u>I'm liking</u> Florence very much. The /
streets are so busy and the people in the streets <u>are</u> always /
<u>smiling</u>. Everybody <u>is loving</u> the Italian way of life. It's so easy- /
going. Bye, <u>I'm having</u> to finish now, because I've got tickets /
for a concert. See you soon, Emma"

Regeln: *simple present*

1. Das ***simple present*** ist die einfache Form der Gegenwart. Du bildest es, indem du ganz einfach die Grundform des Verbs verwendest.
   Beispiele: *He <u>looks</u> good. They <u>learn</u> a lot at school every week. We <u>like</u> this kind of Caribbean music very much.*

2. Das ***simple present*** wird verwendet, wenn eine Handlung immer wieder so abläuft oder ein Zustand immer wieder so eintritt.
   Beispiele: *They <u>go</u> to work early in the morning.*
   (Das taten sie in der Vergangenheit so, tun es in der Gegenwart und werden es in der Zukunft voraussichtlich auch so tun.)
   Fish <u>need</u> water to survive.
   (Das war immer so und wird immer so sein.)

3. Wie du bereits auf Seite 9 erfahren hast, wird in der dritten Person Singular (also bei *he*, *she* und *it*) im ***simple present*** ein -s an das Verb angehängt.
   Beispiel: *We love pop music.* Aber: *<u>He</u> love<u>s</u> pop music.*

Tipp Das *simple present* verwendest du für **Gewohnheiten** und **wiederkehrende** oder **allgemeingültige** Ereignisse. Das kannst du dir mit diesem Merksatz einprägen: **Gewöhne** dich **wieder** an das **Allgemeine**!

Übungen

1 Fülle die Lücken in den folgenden Sätzen mit geeigneten Verben im *simple present*.

a) Paula _________ to church on Sundays twice a month.

b) Don't forget your raincoat. It _________ a lot on the British Isles.

c) Most people _________ that having a big car is too expensive.

d) Most cats don't _________ dogs.

2 Übersetze die folgenden allgemeingültigen Sätze.

a) Fünf mal acht ist 40.

____

b) Die Sonne geht (immer) im Westen unter.

____

c) Wenn man Eis erhitzt, schmilzt es.

____

d) Pflanzen produzieren Sauerstoff (*oxygen*).

____

e) Kinder brauchen Liebe.

____

Regeln: *present progressive*

1. Das ***present progressive*** ist die Verlaufsform der Gegenwart. Es wird nach folgender Regel gebildet:
   Gegenwartsform von *be* + Verb + *-ing*.
   Beispiel: *Where's Peter? He's feeding the guinea pigs in the garden.*

2. Das *present progressive* wird verwendet, wenn eine Handlung gerade stattfindet.
   Beispiel: *Rebecca is reading the newspaper at the moment.*

3. Manchmal bist du dir vielleicht nicht ganz sicher, ob das *simple present* oder das *present progressive* verwendet werden muss. Präge dir hierzu das folgende Schema ein:
   ○ = wiederkehrende Handlung
   ▭ = gerade verlaufende Handlung

simple present: *He gets up early in the morning on workdays.*

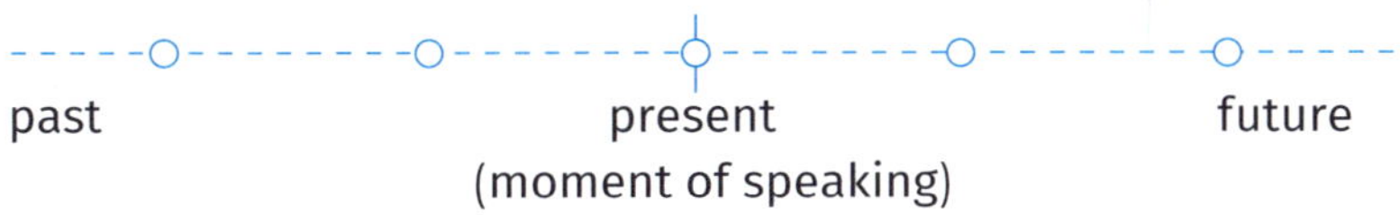

present progressive: *Shhh, be quiet, please, Ma is falling asleep.*

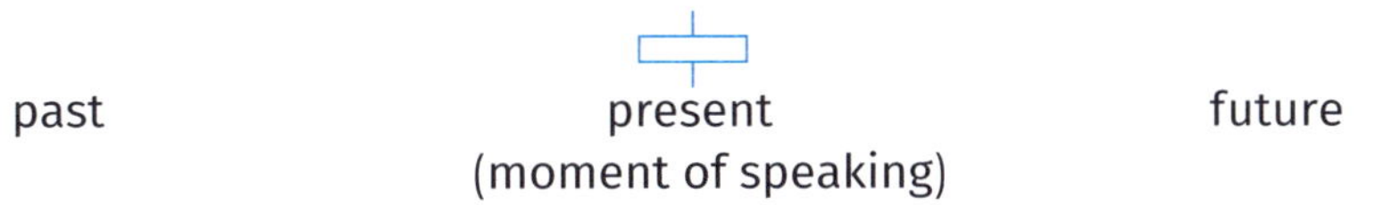

Tipp

Signalwörter für das ***simple present*** sind unter anderen: *sometimes, often, rarely, usually, always, never, frequently.*
Signalwörter für das ***present progressive*** sind unter anderen: *at the moment, (right) now.*

Übungen

3 Bilde aus den folgenden Satzteilen Sätze im *present progressive*. Achte dabei auch auf die richtige Reihenfolge der Wörter.

a) she – some coffee – at the supermarket – buy (.)

____

b) spend – without us – their holidays – this week – they (.)

Can you imagine this? ______________________________

____

c) you – sleep (?) __________________________________

Tipp Achte auf folgende Besonderheiten:

a) Endet die Grundform eines Verbs auf einen Mitlaut (Konsonant) nach kurzem, einfachen und betonten Selbstlaut (Vokal), dann wird dieser Mitlaut in der *progressive*-Form verdoppelt.
Beispiele: *sit → sitting; run → running; stab → stabbing*

b) Wird ein *-e* am Ende der Grundform eines Verbs nicht gesprochen (stummes *-e*), dann fällt es bei der *progressive*-Form weg.
Beispiele: *take → taking; have → having; solve → solving*

4 Trage die richtigen *progressive*-Formen der Verben in Klammern ein.

a) Oh no, look, this young boy is ____________ (have) a beer!

b) The film was good. All the people are ___________ (clap) their hands.

c) Shhh, can you hear this? My brother is ______________ (snore).

d) Oh no! She's really ______________ (sit) next to her English teacher.

5 Im folgenden Bild geschieht gerade sehr viel. Beschreibe die Aktivitäten mithilfe des *present progressive* und der vorgegebenen Satzbruchstücke.

a) The sun ____________________, so it isn't ____________________.

b) Four children ____

____.

c) Three boys ____.

d) A girl ____.

e) Two boys ____.

f) A teacher ____.

g) The school bell ____.

h) A boy ____.

Fehler-Check

Simple present **oder** ***present progressive*****?**

Every Monday evening Joe ______________ (try) to improve his judo skills in the gym. He ____________ (love) this kind of sport because he ______________ (think) it really supports his discipline and his fitness. He usually ______________ (start) his training with fifty sit-ups. Today, however, things are different. Right now he ______________ (sit) in the changing room, because he can't concentrate. He ______________ (dream) about this wonderful young girl. He often ________________ (dream) about girls, although he never ______________ (address) them at school. But this very moment he ______________ (float) on cloud nine, because his heart ______________ (beat) fast and a warm feeling ______________ (run) through his body. Normally he never ______________ (lose) control. This evening, however, his head ______________ (be) like a beehouse. Angels ______________ (sing) wonderful, spheric songs, and magical odours ________________ (pass) by his nose, although he rarely ________________ (care) about perfumes. But what on earth is this? Two strong hands ____________________ (shake) his shoulder, and a loud voice ___________________ (hammer) into his ears. "Hey, _______ you ______________ (sleep)? Wake up! It's time to get to the gym." Oh no, how disillusioning dreams can be!

☐ **Punkte**	**16–19 Punkte**	**9–15 Punkte**	**weniger als 9 Punkte**
	Weltklasse!	Nun ja!	Übe noch einmal!

Simple past oder *past progressive*?

A telephone call

Fred Thomson were having a shower when the phone was ringing. //
He couldn't reach it. That was why he was standing up and /
grabbed his towel. While he stepped out of the tub he was //
slipping on a piece of soap that was lying on the floor. When
he was reaching the phone the ringing was stopping. //

Regeln: *simple past*

1. Das *simple past* ist die einfache Form der Vergangenheit. Bei **regelmäßigen** Verben wird das *simple past* durch Anhängen der Endung ***-ed*** an den Infinitiv (Grundform) des Verbs gebildet.
   Beispiele: *listen → listened; play → played; work → worked*

2. **Achtung:**
   Endet ein regelmäßiges Verb in der Grundform **auf *-y* nach Konsonant**, dann wird aus dem ***-y*** im *simple past* ein ***-ied***.
   Beispiele: *cry → cried; bury → buried;*
   aber: *pray → prayed* (da *-y* nach Vokal, nicht *-y* nach Konsonant)

3. **Achtung:**
   Endet ein regelmäßiges Verb in der Grundform **auf stummem *-e***, dann wird im *simple past* nur noch ein ***-d*** angehängt.
   Beispiel: *like → liked*

4. Die Formen des *simple past* bei **unregelmäßigen Verben** musst du schlicht und einfach lernen. Eine Liste dieser Verben findest du in deinem Englischbuch.
   Beispiele: *see → saw; take → took; read → read; buy → bought*

5. Das *simple past* wird verwendet
   - bei Handlungen und Abläufen, die abgeschlossen in der Vergangenheit liegen,
   - wenn ein Zeitpunkt in der Vergangenheit angegeben ist, z. B. *yesterday, last week, in 1989, two years ago* usw.,
   - bei Fragen mit *when*, die sich auf die Vergangenheit beziehen, z. B. *When did you meet her?*,
   - wenn Handlungen nacheinander in der Vergangenheit abliefen, z. B. *He knocked on my door, came in and sat down on my chair.*

Tipp Bei aufeinanderfolgenden Handlungen in der Vergangenheit findest du häufig Signalwörter wie etwa *first, then, later, suddenly, after that ...*
Beispiel: *First, he brushed his teeth, then he took a shower, after that he got dressed and finally he went down for breakfast.*

Übungen

1 Bilde die *simple-past*-Formen der folgenden Verben. Schlage die unregelmäßigen Verben in deinem Englischbuch nach.

regelmäßige Verben

Grundform	*simple past*
a) play	
b) answer	
c) laugh	
d) turn	
e) talk	
f) need	
g) wait	
h) shout	

unregelmäßige Verben

Grundform	*simple past*
l) come	
m) drive	
n) find	
o) have	
p) make	
q) run	
r) shut	
s) sleep	

i)	like		t)	stand	
j)	help		u)	think	
k)	cry		v)	wear	

Tipp

Merke dir folgende *simple-past*-Formen:
- do → did
- have → had
- be → was/were (I was, you were, he/she/it was, we were, you were, they were)

2 Übertrage die folgenden Sätze ins *simple past*.

a) I have a headache. ______

b) She is twelve. ______

c) They speak Spanish. ______

d) Freddy knows her. ______

e) We like baseball. ______

f) She has breakfast early. ______

g) It rains. ______

h) They laugh a lot. ______

______

Regeln: Verneinungen und Fragen im *simple past*

1. Das *simple past* verneinst du mit *did not* oder seiner Kurzform *didn't*.
   Beispiele: *He worked in Munich.* → *He did not/didn't work in Munich.*
2. Fragen, auf die mit „ja" oder „nein" geantwortet wird, werden mit *did/didn't* gebildet:
   Beispiele: *Did you post the letter? Didn't you know this?*

Übungen

3 Verneine die folgenden Aussagesätze.

a) The two girls reached the exit.

____

b) The old lady was excited.

____

c) She had a wonderful view of London. ______________________________

____

d) They drank much. ______________________________

4 Bilde aus den vier Sätzen der Übung 3) Fragesätze im *simple past*, die mit „ja“ oder „nein“ beantwortet werden können.

a) ______________________________?

b) ______________________________?

c) ______________________________

______________________________?

d) ______________________________?

Regeln: *past progressive*

1. Das *past progressive* (die Verlaufsform der einfachen Vergangenheit) wird mit der Vergangenheitsform von *be* und der *-ing*-Form des Verbs gebildet.
   Beispiel: *I was sitting on the veranda and the sun was shining.*

2. Das *past progressive* wird immer dann verwendet, wenn sich eine Handlung zu einem bestimmten Zeitpunkt in der Vergangenheit im Verlauf befunden hat.
   Beispiel: *When I got up this morning, the sun was shining.*

3. Wenn eine Handlung in der Vergangenheit gerade im Verlauf war (Hintergrundhandlung) und durch eine dazwischenkommende Handlung unterbrochen wird, dann verwendet man für die Hintergrundhandlung das *past progressive*, für die „störende“ Handlung das *simple past*.
Beispiel: *She was watching TV, when suddenly the door bell rang.*

Tipp | Bei Fragen, Kurzantworten und verneinten Sätzen gilt das Gleiche wie im *present progressive*, nur dass eben die Vergangenheitsformen von *be* verwendet werden.
Beispiele: *Were you cooking? – No, I wasn't./I wasn't cooking.*

5 Setze die richtigen Formen des *past progressive* oder *simple past* ein.

a) The old man ______________ (have) a beer, when suddenly a dog ______________(start) to bark.

b) First, I ____________ (finish) my homework, then I __________(go) out.

c) When I ____________ (wake) up in the night, I ____________ (hear) that my brother ________________ (snore).

d) She ___________________ (write) a letter, when there ____________ (be) a knock on the door.

e) He __________________________ (tidy) up his room, when suddenly there ______________ (be) a scream.

f) When they______________ (go) to bed last night, the birds ______________ ______________ (not sing).

Fehler-Check

Simple past oder *past progressive*?

After the summer holidays Mr Roman, the English teacher, ______________________ (ask) the pupils to write a short summary on their holiday activities. Sue ______________ (write): “In the first week my brother and I ________________ (take part) in a summer camp in Wales. On the first day we ________________ (go) to a small village and ________________ (visit) a Roman theatre. The next day we ________________ (go) by bus to a nice lake when we suddenly ________________ (hear) a strange noise. The bus ________________ (stop) and the bus driver ________________ (tell) us that he couldn’t go on with us. So we ________________ (have) to walk the rest of the distance to our camp. The next day we ______________ (try) to cross a river on a raft*. While we ________________ (paddle), Tom ________________ (fall) into the water. We ________________(tear) him out of the water while he ________________ (cry) all the time. On our last day we ________________ (trail down) a lonesome path, when we ________________ (see) Bill, one of the boys, sitting in a tree. A barking dog ________________ (stand) under it. First it ________________ (pull) open the boy’s rucksack and then it ________________ (eat) his lunch.”

☐ **Punkte**	**16–20 Punkte**	**10–15 Punkte**	**weniger als 10 Punkte**
	Hervorragend!	In Ordnung!	Übe noch einmal!

*raft = Floß

Present perfect oder *simple past?*

Were you ever to Scotland? I have spent a wonderful summer holiday last year in the Scottish Highlands. The weather there has been a bit rainy, but every now and then we saw the sun coming out. The Scottish mountains and valleys were just great. We have done a lot of hiking and mountain climbing. When one day we came out of a pub our car was gone. My father has said "Oh my God, somebody stole our car." We were wrong, however. We have just left the pub through the back door.

Regeln

1. Das ***simple past*** bildest du bei regelmäßigen Verben, indem du die Endung *-ed* an die Grundform des Verbs anhängst. Zu den Ausnahmen zu dieser Regel siehe das vorige Kapitel.
   Beispiele: *work → worked; clean → cleaned*
2. Das ***present perfect*** bildest du so:
   have/has + die dritte Form des Verbs.
   Bei regelmäßigen Verben besteht die dritte Form des Verbs aus der Grundform + *-ed*. Bei unregelmäßigen Verben musst du die dritte Form (z. B. *seen, known*) auswendig lernen.
   Beispiele: *He has worked hard for his exam.*
   They have worked hard for their exams.
   Have you seen the clownfish?

Übung

1 Bilde Kurzsätze im *simple past* und im *present perfect*.

	simple past	*present perfect*
I – live – here		
it – rain		
she – see – me		
he – know – her		
we – be – there		
you – have – tea		

Regeln

Das *simple past* und das *present perfect* werden oft falsch verwendet, da ihre Verwendung ein ganz anderes Denken erfordert als im Deutschen.

simple past	*present perfect*
Das *simple past* benutzt du: – für Handlungen und Abläufe, die **abgeschlossen in der Vergangenheit** liegen (oft wird dann ein **Zeitpunkt** angegeben). **Beispiel:** *He bought his car in 2008.* – Wenn Handlungen nacheinander in der Vergangenheit abliefen. **Beispiel:** *He knocked on my door, came in and sat down.*	Das *present perfect* benutzt du: – wenn Handlungen oder Vorgänge in der Vergangenheit begonnen haben und bis zum Zeitpunkt des Sprechens andauern (oft wird dann eine **Zeitdauer** angegeben). **Beispiel:** *She has waited all day.* – wenn Handlungen oder Vorgänge in der Vergangenheit liegen, aber ihr **Ergebnis** zum Zeitpunkt des Sprechens noch sichtbar ist.

Tipp In der Bezeichnung *present perfect* zeigt dir der Wortbestandteil *present*, dass diese Zeitform immer etwas mit der Gegenwart zu tun hat: Entweder dauert eben eine Handlung bis zur Gegenwart an oder das Ergebnis ist für die Gegenwart wichtig. In dem Satz *Have you ever been to Italy?* will der Frager etwa wissen, ob der Gefragte in einem Zeitraum bis jetzt, also jemals, in Italien gewesen ist.

Übung

2 Setze in den folgenden Lücken die richtigen Formen des *present perfect* ein.

a) She ____________ (be) to New York very often. So she ______________ (see) the Statue of Liberty many times in her life.

b) Our teacher _______________ (show) us many films about US national parks this year. Unfortunately, I _______________ (not see) all of them because I was ill for some weeks.

c) Where ____________ you ____________ (be), Tom?

d) What ____________ you ____________ (do), Susan?

e) ____________ she ____________ (read) the book?

f) Sarah can't come. She ________________ (break) her leg.

g) Look! John ________________ (give) me his iPod.

Tipp Typische Signalwörter für das *present perfect* sind:
so far (bis jetzt), *not yet* (noch nicht), *since* (seit: + Zeitpunkt), *for* (seit: + Zeitraum), *up to now* (bis jetzt), *ever* (jemals), *never* (niemals, noch nie), u.a.
Typische Signalwörter für das *simple past* sind:
last year, in 1980, three years ago, last Monday, in the 1990s, in Roman times, u.a.

Übungen

3 Setze *since* oder *for* ein und füge die fehlenden Verbformen ein.

Mary ________________ (wait) for Tom ___________ three hours. She ________________ (not see) him ___________ years, so she's extremely excited. ___________ 2008, when they ________________ (meet) for the first time in Rome, they ________________ (not have) any contact. Oh, there he ______________ (be)! Look at him, he ___________________ (not change). He looks like the young boy Mary ______________ (be) in love with from the first moment they ______________ (see) each other.

4 Übersetze. Verwende das *simple past* und das *present perfect*.

a) Viel hat sich verändert, seitdem ich als Junge hier lebte.

____

____

b) Sie ist seit 2 Jahren arbeitslos *(= unemployed)*.

____

c) Seit 2005 ist mein Vater Mitglied im Volleyballclub. Vor zwei Jahren wurde er Vereinsvorsitzender *(president)*.

____

____

d) Seitdem er letzten Monat nach Boston gereist ist, ist es in unserem Haus ruhig geworden.

____

____

e) (nach einem Lokalbesuch zurück auf der nassen Straße; es regnet nicht) Schau, es hat geregnet.

____

f) (du warst in einem Café auf der Toilette; als du zurückkommst, ist deine Tasse leer) Wer hat meinen Kaffee getrunken?

____

g) Tom hat Mary letzten Dienstag einen Brief geschrieben, aber sie hat ihn nicht erhalten.

____

____

____

____

h) Während meiner Kindheit (= *in my childhood*) habe ich oft große Tiere im Zoo gesehen. Aber so einen großen Bären wie diesen habe ich noch nie gesehen.

____

____

____

____

____

i) (jemand hat deinen Stift weggenommen) Wer hat das getan?

____

Fehler-Check

Kreise die jeweils richtige Zeitform ein.

a) Grace has won/won the song contest last year.

b) How many mails have you written/did you write to him so far?

c) Has he read/Did he read the new Twilight novel?

d) When have you eaten/did you eat sushi for the first time?

e) Since I first have met/met her, I haven't slept/didn't sleep a lot.

f) For so many years people have fought/fought against each other in this African country. But so far politicians have not been/were successful in making peace.

g) Where's Jane? – I don't know. She hasn't arrived/didn't arrive yet.

h) Bill has gone/went to the pop concert last night. I haven't seen/didn't see him since then. He has often been/was often out at night till morning.

i) We have bought/bought our car in 2008, but since then our neighbours have bought/bought three cars.

j) Has he told/Did he tell you about my secret? Really? When has he done/did he do this?

k) Son, tell me. How often have you had/did you have a beer so far?

l) I'm really exhausted. My mother has talked/talked to me for hours.

☐ **Punkte**	**15–18 Punkte** Super!	**9–14 Punkte** In Ordnung!	**weniger als 9 Punkte** Bitte noch einmal üben!

Irregular verbs – richtig verwendet

Emma has be to Switzerland for several times in her life, that's /
why she known how to behave when suddenly some cows are /
running after you. On that sunny day last Tuesday she first want /
to stand still and be quiet. But when one of the cows come closer /
to her, she becames frightened and started running. But in the end /
she blown the whistle she was carrying with her, and the cow /
turn round and runs off. //

Regeln

In vielen Englischbüchern findest du **eine Liste der unregelmäßigen Verben** mit ihren Formen. Meist ist eine solche Liste wie folgt aufgebaut:

Infinitiv	*past-tense*-Form	Perfekt-Form	deutsch
see	saw	seen	sehen/sah/gesehen
think	thought	thought	denken/dachte/gedacht
go	went	gone	gehen/ging/gegangen
buy	bought	bought	kaufen/kaufte/gekauft
…	…	…	…

Denke daran, dass die zweite Form (z. B. *saw, thought*) einzig und allein im *simple past* verwendet wird. Die dritte Form (z. B. *seen, thought*) entspricht der Verbform, die im Deutschen meist mit *ge-* beginnt, also *gesehen, gedacht*. Sie wird nur für die Perfekt-Formen verwendet, von denen du allerdings erst das *present perfect* kennst. Achte aber bitte genau darauf, wann du das *present perfect* verwenden kannst. Man kann nämlich nicht sagen, dass beispielsweise der deutsche Satz *Ich habe am Montag dieses Buch gelesen* im Englischen mit ~~*I have read this book on Monday*~~ wiedergegeben wird, ganz im Gegenteil, das wäre falsch, denn es muss heißen *I read this book on Monday*. Schaue dir hierzu noch einmal die vorhergehenden Kapitel in diesem Buch an, die sich mit den verschiedenen *tenses* befassen.

Tipp Im ersten Lernjahr wirst du es hauptsächlich mit den ersten beiden Spalten (Infinitiv und *past-tense*-Form) zu tun haben. Besser ist es trotzdem, wenn du nach Möglichkeit gleich alle drei Formen des unregelmäßigen Verbs lernst.

Übung

1 Setze ein.

Infinitiv	*past-tense*-Form	Perfekt-Form	deutsch
tell			
	ran		
		stolen	
			machen
		got	
	caught		
swim			
	fought		
		known	
			bringen
		read	
	taught		

write			
	took		
		kept	
			fahren

Tipp Bei den **regelmäßigen** Verben entspricht die *past-tense*-Form (Spalte 2) auch immer der Perfekt-Form (Spalte 3), also z. B. *listen – listened – listened, want – wanted – wanted.*

Übung

2 Setze in die folgenden Lücken die richtigen Formen der unregelmäßigen Verben ein.

a) Lara __________ (go) to New Zealand two weeks ago.

b) Have you ever __________ (eat) a plumcake?

c) Last month Pete __________ (meet) his mother in Los Angeles.

d) She hasn't __________ (buy) a new scarf so far. She still uses her old one.

e) No, I didn't __________ (lose) my MP3-Player on Wednesday. I have never __________ (lose) anything in my life.

f) You can easily translate this German movie title into English. „Die vergessene Welt" in English is "The ____________________ World".

g) She _______________ (catch) the ball with one hand.

h) Yesterday I __________ (swim) in the lake.

i) When he __________ (see) that the police were coming in his direction he quickly __________ (run) away.

j) While she was working as an au pair in Washington she __________ (keep) in touch with her family via Skype.

Fehler-Check

Setze die richtigen englischen Verbformen ein.

a) Although she was very exhausted after the concert, the pop star ________ (give) an interview and ______________ (answer) all the questions.

b) Did they really ________ (sell) their house last year?

c) Picasso ________ (make) this painting shortly before he died.

d) Has your team ever ________ (beat) our team?

e) Where's my pencil-case? Somebody has ________ (steal) it!

f) He doesn't ________ (teach) Latin, but he has __________ (teach) Maths for years, and he has __________ (be) quite a good teacher.

g) My aunt always __________ (know) how to tell a good joke.

h) I've ________ (wait) for you since 9 o'clock. Where have you ________ (be)?

i) ________ (tell) me what she ________ (say) yesterday.

j) We didn't ________ (know) much about the Italian language, so we ____________ (fetch) a German-Italian dictionary.

k) He ________ (be) 16 when he ________ (meet) her for the first time.

☐ **Punkte**	**14–18 Punkte** Super!	**8–13 Punkte** In Ordnung!	**weniger als 8 Punkte** Bitte noch einmal üben!

Going to future oder *will future?*

Amy is going to be thirteen next Thursday. She will invite all her friends, so she has already made plans and prepared invitation cards. There is going to be good music, and, as every year, her neighbours are going to complain. Amy thinks they are going to talk to her parents after the party. That's why Amy will invite them.

Regeln: *going to future*

1. Das *going to future* ist eine von mehreren Möglichkeiten, zukünftige Ereignisse/Handlungen auszudrücken. Du bildest das *going to future* folgendermaßen:
   Form von *be* + *going to* + Grundform (Infinitiv) des Verbs.
   Beispiele: *Freddy is going to finish his final paper tomorrow.*
   They are going to get a new car soon.

2. Das *going to future* verwendet man für zukünftige Ereignisse, die sich bereits durch deutliche **Anzeichen** ankündigen.
   Beispiele: *Oh, there are dark clouds in the sky. It's going to rain soon.*
   Watch out, we're going to crash!

3. Außerdem verwendet man das *going to future*, um **Pläne** für die Zukunft auszudrücken. Es geht dabei um **feste Vorhaben**, für die gegebenenfalls auch schon Vorbereitungen laufen.
   Beispiele: *We're going to have a great party next Saturday, we have already invited all our friends.*
   I'm going to fly to Belfast.

Übungen

1 Bilde Sätze mit *going to future*.

a) Take an umbrella. It ____________________ . (rain)

b) The plane is rolling to the runway. It ____________________. (take off)

c) She's bought a ticket at the counter. She ____________________ (take) the bus to Memphis.

2 Bilde aus den folgenden Aussagesätzen Fragesätze, auf die mit „ja“ oder „nein“ geantwortet werden kann.

a) He's going to have driving lessons.

____

b) She's going to have a baby next month.

____

c) You're going to pack your suitcase.

____

d) They are going to leave the country in an hour.

____

e) I'm going to get my hair cut.

____

Regeln: *will future*

1. Das *will future* wird ganz einfach gebildet:
   will + Grundform (Infinitiv) des Verbs.
   Beispiele: *I <u>will help</u> you. Who <u>will win</u> the finals?*

2. Das *will future* wird verwendet, wenn man **Vorhersagen** oder **Vermutungen** über die Zukunft zum Ausdruck bringen will.
   Beispiele: *Sven <u>will be</u> twenty next month. I think she <u>will be</u> proud.*

3. Darüber hinaus gebraucht man das *will future*, wenn man sich **spontan für etwas entscheidet** oder **spontan eine Reaktion äußert**.
   Beispiele: *Wait, I <u>will pick up</u> your brother at the station.*
   OK, I think <u>I'll have</u> the chicken burger then.

Tipp | Merke dir für den Gebrauch des *will future* folgende Signalwörter:
I think, I'm sure, I suppose, maybe, perhaps, probably.

Übung

3 Betty ist bei ihrer Gastfamilie in Texas angekommen. Sie ist noch etwas nervös und stellt deshalb einige Vermutungen an.

a) She thinks ____.

(... dass ihre Gastmutter *(host mother)* streng sein wird.)

b) Maybe ____.

(... wird sie ihr Zimmer nicht mögen.)

c) She __________ probably ______________________________.

(... wird wahrscheinlich Probleme mit der Sprache haben.)

d) She's sure ____.

(... dass sie die Kinder mögen wird.)

e) Perhaps ____.

(... wird sie das amerikanische Essen hassen.)

Fehler-Check

***Going to future* oder *will future*?**

a) I think the team ________________ win next Saturday.

b) Oh, I've dropped the matches. – No problem, I ________________ get you new ones.

c) She's pregnant. She ________________ have her baby in April.

d) The sun ________________ set at 6.30 tomorrow. But we ________________ watch the sunset, because the weather forecast is horrible.

e) Pete is worried about his English test. ________________ he succeed?

f) Watch out, this firecracker ________________ explode!

g) My grandpa ________________ be 70 next week. That's why we ________________ have a big family party on Sunday. What ________________ the weather be like? 'High Edmund' is approaching from the Atlantic. There ________________ be sunshine.

h) Next Monday ________________ be May 1st. So there ________________ be a holiday.

i) ________________ spend your next holiday in Ireland?

j) What would you like to have for dinner? – I think I ________________ take a soup first.

k) She's sure that her brother ________________ be back soon.

☐ Punkte	13–16 Punkte	8–12 Punkte	weniger als 8 Punkte
	Super!	In Ordnung!	Bitte noch einmal üben!

Fehlerquelle Adjektiv und Adverb

4

Adjektive richtig steigern und vergleichen

I've got a strange pet at home. It's more big than a cat, but /
smaller as a sheep. It is not the most old pet I have, because //
it's more young than my dog Cesar. This pet is activer than my //
two white mice at night. It sleeps in a more big cage. It simply is /
an animal as strange than a unicorn. However, it's beautifuller //
than a unicorn. My pet is a dragonwolve.

Regeln

1. Bei der Steigerung von Adjektiven unterscheidet man drei Formen:
   a) **Positiv** (ungesteigert, z. B. *cheap*)
   b) **Komparativ** (erste Steigerung, z. B. *cheaper*)
   c) **Superlativ** (zweite Steigerung, z. B. *cheapest*)
2. Einsilbige Adjektive werden so gesteigert:
   Komparativ (*comparative*): Anhängen von ***-er***: *old → older*
   Superlativ (*superlative*): Anhängen von ***-est***: *old → oldest*
3. Zweisilbige Adjektive auf *-y, -le, -er, -ow* werden ebenfalls mit *-er* und *-est* gesteigert.
   Beispiele: *simple → simpler → simplest*
   slow → slower → slowest
   clever → cleverer → cleverest
4. Alle anderen Adjektive steigert man mit vorangestelltem *more* im Komparativ und *most* im Superlativ.
   Beispiele: *wonderful → more wonderful → most wonderful*
   solemn (feierlich) *→ more solemn → most solemn*
   intelligent → more intelligent → most intelligent

Übung

1 Bestimme die folgenden Steigerungsformen: Positiv (P), Komparativ (K) oder Superlativ (S).

a) stupid:

b) richest:

c) quicker:

d) more fantastic:

e) most dangerous:

f) faster:

g) heaviest:

h) strong:

i) more individual:

j) bigger:

Regeln

Achtung: Bei manchen Adjektiven ändert sich bei der Steigerung die Schreibweise.

1. Bei Adjektiven, die auf **-y** enden, wird das **-y** in der Steigerung zu **-*i***.
Beispiele: *happy → happier → happiest*

2. Und noch eine Besonderheit: Bei Adjektiven, die nach kurzem Vokal auf einen Konsonanten enden, wird dieser Konsonant beim Steigern verdoppelt.
Beispiele: *fat → fatter → fattest; big → bigger → biggest*

Übung

2 Bilde die fehlenden Formen für die folgenden Adjektive.

Positiv	Komparativ	Superlativ
	shorter	
industrious (fleißig)		
		curliest

		most interesting
	noisier	
		noblest
hip		

Tipp Eine typische Fehlerquelle sind die folgenden beiden Sonderformen der Steigerung, die du einfach auswendig lernen musst:
good – better – best *bad – worse – worst*

Regeln

Oft wird mithilfe von Adjektiven verglichen. Dabei gelten zwei Regeln:

1. Bei **Ungleichheit**, also wenn etwas z. B. größer/älter/schneller ist, gilt: **Komparativform + *than***.
   Beispiel: *This new car is faster than the old one.*
2. Bei **Gleichheit**, also wenn etwas z. B. genauso groß/alt/schnell ist, gilt: **... *as* + Positivform + *as* ...**
   Beispiel: *This new car is as fast as the old one.*

Übung

3 *Mediation*: Übertrage die folgenden Sprechabsichten ins Englische.

a) Bringe zum Ausdruck, dass dies die teuerste Zeitung ist.

____

b) Frage Ella, ob sie so alt wie dein Bruder ist.

____

c) Beschimpfe Alan. Sage ihm, er sei der dümmste Junge auf Erden.

____

Fehler-Check

Setze die fehlenden Adjektiv- und Vergleichsformen ein.

My house is _________________ *(größer als)* my neighbour's . I'm sure my house is the _______________ *(größte)* building in our street. Although my sports car is _______________ *(nicht so schnell wie)* John's, it is the ________ *(schnellste)* car I've ever had. To be honest, it's even __________________ ___________ *(teurer als)* a Ferrarri. I'm really not a _____________ *(dumm)* blowhard *(Angeber)*, but the _______________ *(schlechteste)* thing you can do is give people the idea that they are ______________ *(besser)* than you. That's why I always wear the _____________________ *(coolsten)* clothes I can get. Sometimes I also love _____________ *(gutes)* fast food, but what I think is the _____________ *(großartigste)* feeling, is going out for ___________ *(fein)* dinners in the __________________ *(berühmtesten)* restaurant in town. I'm a bit _____________ *(schüchtern)* sometimes, although I have paid a lot of money to my psychiatrist, who, by the way, is one of the _______________ *(besten)* in our country. In my ___________ *(letzte)* session with him, I asked him why I haven't found a nice girl so far. He just said: "Tom, you are the _______________ *(netteste)* man on earth!"

☐ **Punkte**	**14–17 Punkte**	**8–13 Punkte**	**weniger als 8 Punkte**
	Hervorragend!	In Ordnung!	Übe noch einmal!

Adverbien richtig platzieren

Cathy is spending in Wales her summer holiday. She arrived /
yesterday at the station, where Uncle Sam picked up her. //
She has been never to Wales, so asks she Uncle Sam to show her //
in the west the nice beaches. Uncle Sam tells patiently her about //
Welsh history, but Cathy is too tired to listen to carefully him. /

Regeln: Adverbien der Häufigkeit

1. Adverbien der Häufigkeit *(adverbs of frequency)* geben an, **wie oft** etwas getan wird.
   Beispiele: *often, sometimes, never, always, rarely, regularly, frequently, normally*

2. Diese Adverbien stehen im Satz **vor** dem Vollverb und **nach** dem Hilfsverb bzw. einer Form von *be*.
   Beispiele: *We sometimes light a candle in the evening.*
   She has often told us good-night stories.
   You are always late. She has always been late.

Übung

1 Markiere die richtige Position der Adverbien der Häufigkeit mit einem farbigen, senkrechten Strich.

a) Jan works until late at night. (often)
b) She has been in Paris. (never)
c) We go to the zoo late in the afternoon. (sometimes)
d) He's excited before tests. (always)
e) They help their father in the garden. (regularly)

Regeln: Adverbien der Art und Weise

1. Adverbien der Art und Weise *(adverbs of manner)* geben an, auf welche Art und Weise, also **wie** eine Handlung durchgeführt wird.
   Beispiel: *She brushed her hair slowly.*

2. Adverbien der Art und Weise bildet man, indem man die Endung ***-ly*** an das Adjektiv anhängt.
   Beispiel: *clever/enormous/beautiful → cleverly/enormously/beautifully*

3. Beachte folgende Sonderfälle:
   - Endet das Adjektiv auf ***-y* nach Konsonant**, dann endet das dazugehörige Adverb auf ***-ily***.
     Beispiel: *angry → angrily; busy → busily*
   - Endet das Adjektiv auf ***-ic***, dann endet das Adverb auf ***-ically***.
     Beispiel: *basic → basically*
   - Endet das Adjektiv auf ein stummes ***-e* nach *l***, dann entfällt das stumme ***-e*** bei der Adverb-Bildung.
     Beispiel: *simple → simply*
   - Das Adverb zum Adjektiv ***good*** lautet ***well***.

Tipp Bei Adjektiven, die schon auf *-ly* enden, benutzt man in der Adverbkonstruktion die Umschreibungen *in a ... way/manner.*
Beispiel: *He answered the question in a lovely way/manner.*

Übungen

2 Bilde zu den folgenden Adjektiven die Adverbien der Art und Weise.

Adjektiv	Adverb
horrible	
silly	
extreme	
mad	
friendly	

easy	
quiet	
good	

3 Adjektiv oder Adverb? Streiche die jeweils falsche Form durch.

Last Tuesday Jimmy had his first/firstly French test at school. When he entered his classroom he was calm/calmly. But when he got his paper, he started to laugh furious/furiously*. His teacher said: "You have to be absolute/absolutely quiet/quietly, Jimmy! Listen, all the others are working quiet/quietly. They can't concentrate proper/properly." But Jimmy couldn't stop laughing, so he left the room quick/quickly.

*furious = wild

Regeln: Satzstellung von Adverbien der Art und Weise

Adverbien der Art und Weise stehen an verschiedenen Positionen im Satz:

a) **vor** dem Vollverb: *Paul can easily do this job. She quickly got up.*

b) **am Ende** des Satzes: *Mia can speak Spanish well.*

c) **nach** dem Objekt, jedoch **vor** einem weiteren Adverb oder einer adverbialen Bestimmung des Ortes oder der Zeit.
She played her trumpet loudly in his room until 10 o'clock.

Tipp Ein Adverb der Art und Weise steht nie zwischen Verb und Objekt.
FALSCH: ~~He brushed quickly his teeth~~.
RICHTIG: He brushed his teeth quickly.

Übung

4 Markiere die richtige Position der Adverbien der Art und Weise mit einem farbigen, senkrechten Strich.

a) My cat Tabby was eating her food. (hungrily)
b) Leon, the lion, was sitting on the sofa. (lazily)
c) Maxwell, my chameleon, was looking at me. (patiently)

d) Homer, the bulldog, was running into the kitchen. (hastily)
e) Cleopatra, the spider, was watching 'Spiderman' in the living-room until midnight. (happily)
f) Ramses, the dromedary, was waiting in the bathroom. (nervously)

Regeln: Adverbien des Ortes und der Zeit

1. Adverbien und adverbiale Bestimmungen des Ortes und der Zeit *(adverbs/adverbials of time and place)* sind zum Beispiel: *yesterday, two weeks ago, in 2001, every day, under the tree, in the garden, in Stuttgart, into the house.*

2. Für die Stellung im Satz gilt: **Ort vor Zeit, Richtung vor Ort** sowie **Genaueres vor Allgemeinerem**, z. B. Uhrzeit vor Tag, Straße vor Stadtviertel.
Beispiel: *Tom left his office in Wall Street at 9 o'clock in the evening.*

Übungen

5 Bilde Sätze aus den folgenden Bruchstücken. Achte auf die richtige Reihenfolge der Wörter.

a) Mary – until late in the morning – the newspaper – in the dining-room – was reading.

____

____

b) when – into the chapel – she came – she saw – in the centre – of a pool – a statue

____

____

c) through the garden gate – something dark – came – at midnight

____

____

d) he – on Sundays – his friend – met – in the churchyard – often – at 10 o'clock

____

____

e) Mary-Lou – drove home – slowly – last Monday – from the snackbar

____

____

6 Übertrage die folgenden Sätze ins Englische.

a) Viele Menschen reisen jeden Sommer an die Küsten in Großbritannien.

____

____

b) Oft besuchen sie die wundervollen alten Kirchen in den Dörfern im Osten.

____

____

c) Sie gehen manchmal in den Läden in der Hauptstraße bis spät abends einkaufen.

____

____

d) Dort kann man in den Regalen immer viele Souvenire finden.

____

____

Fehler-Check

Setze das Wort in Klammern an die richtige Stelle im Satz.

a) I ____________ haven't ____________ been ____________ for ages. (in Britain)

b) He ________ answered ________ the ________ question. (quickly)

c) He answered ____________ the ____________ question ____________. (angrily)

d) They're ________ late ________ for ________ work. (often)

e) Tom really ____________ behaves ____________ at the moment ____________. (stupidly)

f) My father ____________ likes ____________ going ____________ for a walk. (sometimes)

g) Have ________ you ________ been ________ to London? (ever)

h) She's got ____________ twenty cats ____________ in Brighton ____________. (in her house)

i) Mrs Thomson ____________ often ____________ cleans ____________. (all the windows)

j) They ______________ cared about ______________ his little dog ______________. (in a lovely way)

☐ **Punkte**	**8–10 Punkte** Hervorragend!	**5–7 Punkte** In Ordnung!	**weniger als 5 Punkte** Übe noch einmal!

Satzkonstruktionen: systematisch richtig!

Imperatives und *modal auxiliaries*

Hey, son, tidies up your room! Don't sitting around! You need show III
me that you are a big boy. You mustn't clean your room every day, I
but you can follow my instructions. I mustn't understand why you II
are so lazy. So, come on, doesn't lie around! I

Regeln: Imperative *(imperatives)*

1. Imperativformen werden verwendet, um eine Aufforderung direkt an die angesprochene Person zu richten. Man kann jemanden auffordern, etwas zu tun (**Befehlssätze**). Man kann aber auch jemanden auffordern, etwas zu unterlassen (**Verbotssätze**).
   Beispiele: *Sit down! Don't look around!*
2. Befehlssätze bildest du mit der Grundform (Infinitiv) des Verbs.
   Beispiele: *Open your books! Close the window! Stop talking!*
3. Verbotssätze bildest du so:
   don't + Grundform (Infinitiv) des Verbs.
   Beispiele: *Don't talk! Don't sit on your desks! Don't sleep!*

Übung

1 Übersetze die folgenden Befehle/Anweisungen und Verbote.

a) Schreib nicht in dein Buch!

____

b) Nimm deinen Finger aus dem Mund!

____

c) Öffne das Fenster!

____

d) Geh mir nicht auf die Nerven!

____

e) Steh nicht herum, arbeite!

____

Regeln: Modale Hilfsverben *(modal auxiliaries)*

Mit **modalen Hilfsverben** kannst du ausdrücken, was man kann/darf/muss/soll oder nicht soll. Modale Hilfsverben benötigen immer zusätzlich ein **Vollverb in der Grundform** (Infinitiv).
Beispiele: *I can speak English. She must go home. He need not help.*

Die Tabelle zeigt die **Verwendungsmöglichkeiten** modaler Hilfsverben:

Hilfsverb	Verwendung	Deutsch/Englisch
can *cannot/can't*	Fähigkeit/Unfähigkeit, etwas zu tun	Sie kann (nicht) sprechen. → *She can (can't) speak.*
can *cannot/can't*	Bitte um Erlaubnis	Kann/Darf er sich hinsetzen? → *Can he sit down?*
must *doesn't/ don't have to*	Notwendigkeit, Nicht-Notwendigkeit	Ich muss gehen. → *I must go.* Ich muss nicht gehen. → *I don't have to go.*
have to *doesn't/ don't have to*	Ersatzform von must	Wir müssen (nicht) arbeiten. → *We (don't) have to work.*
must not/ mustn't	!!! Verbot !!!	Du darfst nicht mit Fremden reden. → *You mustn't talk to strangers.*
need not/ needn't	fehlende Notwendigkeit	Ich brauche es ihr nicht zu sagen. → *I needn't tell her.*

Übungen

2 Übersetze.

Du kannst diesen Roman *(= novel)* haben und du darfst heute die ersten zwanzig Seiten lesen. Du brauchst dafür nichts zu bezahlen. Aber du musst das Buch am Abend ins Regal stellen.

____

____

____

____

____

3 Setze die passenden Modalhilfsverben ein:

can ▪ can't ▪ can't ▪ don't have to ▪ have to ▪ must ▪ mustn't ▪ needn't

a) My sister ____________ swim. She has never been taught how to swim.

b) ____________ you help me, please? I ____________ finish this puzzle without you.

c) ____________ I really lay the table? – No, you needn't.

d) Pupils ____________ be in their classroom during breaks.

e) You ________________ tell me, I already know the story.

f) Oh, it's late, I ____________ go home now.

g) You ________________ help me. I will get along without you.

Fehler-Check

Kreuze die richtigen Sätze an. Für jede richtige Antwort erhältst du einen Punkt.

a) You must stop here. ☐
b) You needn't stop here. ☐
c) You have to stop here. ☐

d) You mustn't go straight on. ☐
e) You have to turn right. ☐
f) You must turn right. ☐

g) You can go straight on. ☐
h) You can't turn left. ☐
i) You mustn't turn right. ☐

j) You mustn't stop here. ☐
k) You can't stop here. ☐
l) You have to go on. ☐

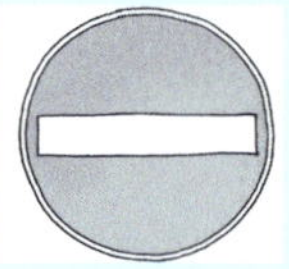

m) You mustn't enter this road. ☐
n) You don't have to enter this road. ☐
o) You cannot enter this road. ☐

☐ Punkte

8–9 Punkte Hervorragend!
4–7 Punkte In Ordnung!
weniger als 4 Punkte Übe noch einmal!

Conditional sentences

A girl to her boyfriend

If you don't bring me flowers every day, I am angry with you. If you /
would love me, you would always be nice to me. And I will love you /
forever if you went to the cinema with me every Saturday. If I see that /
you look at other girls, I would leave you. And if you lie to me, I become //
a horrible beast.

Regeln

Im Englischen gibt es drei Arten von **Bedingungssätzen** *(conditional sentences)*. Die ersten beiden (***type I*** und ***type II***) lernst du in diesem Kapitel kennen.

1. Bedingungssätze bestehen immer aus einem sogenannten *if-clause* und einem Hauptsatz *(main clause)*. Der *if-clause* nennt eine Bedingung. Der Hauptsatz gibt an, was geschieht, wenn die Bedingung erfüllt oder nicht erfüllt wird.
2. Im ***conditional sentence type I*** ist die Bedingung grundsätzlich **erfüllbar** und **wahrscheinlich**.
   Im *if-clause* des Typ I verwendet man das *simple present*.
   Im Hauptsatz des Typ I verwendet man das *will future*.
   Beispiele: *If she comes, I will be happy.*
   → Wenn sie kommt, bin ich glücklich.
3. Es ist egal, ob der *if-clause* oder der Hauptsatz vorne steht. Wichtig ist nur: Steht der *if-clause* vorne, dann wird dieser mit einem **Komma** vom folgenden Hauptsatz abgetrennt. Steht dagegen der Hauptsatz vorne, wird kein Komma gesetzt.
   Beispiele: *If it rains, I will stay in bed. I will stay in bed if it rains.*

Tipp | Denk daran: Kein *would* oder *should* im *if-clause*!

Übungen

1 Setze die Verben in der richtigen Zeitform ein.

a) If you ______________ (not do) this exercise,
you ________________ (not pass) the test.

b) You ______________ (not be) hungry this evening
if you ______________ (eat) so much chocolate.

c) If you ______________ (not stop) phoning,
I ______________ (tear) the plug.

d) If you ______________ (be) that nervous in the test,
you ______________ (make) a lot of mistakes.

e) You ______________ (miss) the film if you ____________ (not hurry).

2 Ergänze die folgenden Sätze nach deinen eigenen Vorstellungen.
Achte auf die richtige Zeitform.

a) If they travel to Paris in summer, ________________________________
____

b) She will be very angry if _____________________________________
____

c) If he doesn't get an answer, __________________________________
____

d) Mr Miller won't buy the car if _________________________________
____

Regeln

1. Beim Bedingungssatz **Typ II** *(type II)* wird eine Bedingung genannt, die **wahrscheinlich nicht erfüllt** werden kann. Stelle dir folgende Situation vor: Deine Freundin hat dir gesagt, dass es für sie sehr schwierig wird, zu deiner Party zu kommen. Im unwahrscheinlichen Fall, dass sie doch käme, würdest du dich freuen:
   If she came, I would be happy. → Wenn sie käme, wäre ich glücklich.

2. Im *if-clause* des Typ II verwendet man das *simple past*. Im Hauptsatz des Typ II verwendet man das *conditional* (*would* + Infinitiv).
   Beispiel: *She would come to the party if she had a car.*

Übung

3 *Gold fever.* Setze die Verben in der richtigen Zeitform ein.

a) If you ______________ (tell) me the secret, I ______________ (not tell) anybody.

b) I ______________ (find) the treasure if you ______________ (give) me the map.

c) If I ______________ (find) the gold, I ______________ (give) you half of it.

d) If I ______________ (have) my gold, I ______________ (not get) on your nerves any longer.

e) I ______________ (buy) a new play station if I ______________ (get) much money for my gold.

f) I ______________ (not go) to school any longer if I ______________ (be) rich.

Fehler-Check

Setze die richtigen Verbformen ein.

a) If Tim __________ (join) our team, we would win the next match.

b) Tina will be able to go shopping with us later if she _________ (do) her homework now.

c) If you lose your passport, you ___________________ (have to) go to the police.

d) If she loved me, she _______________ (tell) me.

e) We would buy a house if we ___________ (have) 300 000 €.

f) If Mary ___________ (save) more money, she could go to the concert.

g) If he knew the effects of alcoholism, he __________________ (not drink) so much.

h) I would help her if she __________ (ask) me.

i) If John doesn't improve his English skills, he _____________ (fail) his exam.

j) If people _________ (know) more about this virus, they would be careful.

k) She won't be happy if you ________ (tell) her the truth.

l) If I _________ (be) a pilot, I would like to fly the Airbus.

m) If I _________________ (be asked), I would like to be a pilot.

n) Your cat will become aggressive if you _____________ (grap) her tail.

o) If you ____________________ (not accept) this offer, you would be silly.

☐ **Punkte**	**12–15 Punkte** Hervorragend!	**7–11 Punkte** In Ordnung!	**weniger als 7 Punkte** Übe noch einmal!

Who und *what*

What said you? – I didn't say anything. – But somebody said something! Who did something say? – Nobody said anything. Whose voice heard you? – I don't know. Who did say something? – Nobody did. Whose your doctor? – Dr Stevenson. – Then go and see him!

Regeln

Fragesätze mit den Fragewörtern *who*, *whose* und *what* werden sehr oft falsch gebildet.

1. ***Who*** bedeutet entweder *wer*, *wen* oder *wem*.
   Beispiele: *Who won the competition yesterday?* (Wer ...?)
   Who did you meet yesterday? (Wen ...?)
   Who did she write an email last Monday? (Wem ...?)
2. ***Whose*** als Fragewort bedeutet *wessen*. Achtung: Verwechsle *whose* nicht mit *who's* (wer ist).
   Beispiel: *Whose book is this?* (Wessen Buch ist das?)

Übung

1 *A car accident.*
Setze in die folgenden Lücken *who*, *whose* oder *who's* ein.

a) ________ did you see at the corner shortly after the accident?

b) ________ car came from the right?

c) ________ the driver of the black car?

d) ________ has called the police?

e) ________ bike is this?

Regeln

Who und ***what*** können nach dem Subjekt oder dem Objekt fragen.

1. Frage nach dem **Subjekt** (Wer oder was?):
   Who stole the bike? → Wer ...?
   What caused the accident? → Was ...?
   Hier wird **keine Umschreibung mit *do*** vorgenommen!

2. Frage nach dem **Objekt** (Wen/Wem oder was?):
   Who did he meet? → Wen ...?
   Who did she give the book? → Wem ...?
   What did he say? → Was ...?
   Hier ist eine **Umschreibung mit *do*** zwingend notwendig!

Übungen

2 Übertrage die folgenden Fragen ins Englische.

a) Wen liebt sie? ______

b) Wer liebt sie? ______

c) Was liebt er? ______

d) Wen mochte er? ______

e) Was sagtet ihr? ______

f) Wem vertraust du? ______

g) Was half ihm? ______

h) Wer bist du? ______

i) Wer kennt dich? ______

j) Was ist das? ______

k) Wen siehst du? ______

l) Wem schreibt sie? ______

Tipp Achtung: Das englische Fragewort *who* hat nichts mit dem deutschen Fragewort *wo* zu tun!
Beispiele: *Who's the guy with the green shirt?*
→ Wer ist der Typ mit dem grünen Shirt?
Where's the guy with the green shirt?
→ Wo ist der Typ mit dem grünen Shirt?

3 Entscheide, welche der beiden Varianten jeweils richtig ist. Streiche die falsche Variante durch.

a) – Who told you this story?
– Who did tell you this story?

b) – Who met you in Munich yesterday?
– Who did you meet in Munich yesterday?

c) – What did you answer to this silly question?
– What answered you to this silly question?

d) – What did the damage cause?
– What caused the damage?

e) – Who wrote he so many letters?
– Who did he write so many letters?

f) – What did she see?
– What saw she?

g) – What do you think?
– What think you?

h) – Who protested against the new station building?
– Who did protest against the new station building?

i) – Who did say that teachers had to be strict?
– Who said that teachers had to be strict?

Fehler-Check

Füge ein: *who, who's, whose, what* und die fehlenden Formen von *do*.

I'm a little zebra and I'm new here at the Blackwood Zoo. So I've got many questions to ask: ________ will give me my water? _______ the owner of this zoo? ________ must I do to get enough food? Who _______ I have to tell if I feel sick? What _______ I do after a heavy thunderstorm*? ________ this strange man in the white coat? What _______ "vet" mean? ________ child is this next to the kiosk? What _______ all the animals do at night? ________ will tell me bedtime stories? _______ tells me where to get my food in the morning? Who _________ I have to ask about toys? _________ do I have for breakfast? ________ tells me about sport activities? ________ do I have to ask for new clothes? _______ responsible for lessons in how to annoy lions? _________ will happen, if I don't go to the zoo school? ________ vehicle can I use when I would like to go on a trip outside the zoo? ________ gives me information about holiday camps in Africa?

☐ Punkte	15–19 Punkte	9–14 Punkte	weniger als 9 Punkte
	Hervorragend!	In Ordnung!	Übe noch einmal!

*thunderstrom = Gewitter

Relative clauses

The girl who's dog is named Homer is twelve. She lives in the house /
in York Road what is painted blue. Her father, that is an engineer, //
loves dogs, too. That's why he'd like to have another dog, one of those
who usually herd sheep. He is one of the people which love running and //
these sheepdogs love running as well.

Regeln: Notwendige und nicht notwendige Relativsätze

1. Ein Relativsatz (*relative clause*) ist ein Nebensatz, der ergänzende Informationen zu Personen oder Dingen enthält, die im Hauptsatz erwähnt sind.
   Beispiele: *The man who lives next to us plays the piano.*
   Mr Johnson, who is fifty-five, is a dentist.

2. Im Englischen gibt es notwendige und nicht notwendige Relativsätze. Ein **notwendiger Relativsatz** enthält eine Information, die notwendig ist, um die Aussage im Hauptsatz überhaupt zu verstehen. So ein Relativsatz steht **niemals zwischen Kommas**, weil er für den Hauptsatz so wichtig ist.
   Beispiel: *The man who lives next to us plays the piano.*
   (Hieße der Satz nur „*The man plays the piano*“, wüsste man nicht, um welchen Mann es sich handelt.)

3. Im **nicht notwendigen** Relativsatz steht eine zusätzliche Information, die zum Verständnis des Hauptsatzes nicht notwendig ist. So ein Relativsatz wird immer **mit Kommas vom Hauptsatz abgetrennt**.
   Beispiel: *Mr Johnson, who is fifty-five, is a dentist.*
   (Die Kernaussage im Hauptsatz, dass nämlich Mr Johnson ein Zahnarzt ist, ist auch ohne die Altersangabe im Relativsatz klar.)

Übungen

1 Welche der folgenden Relativsätze sind notwendig, welche sind nicht notwendig? Kreuze an.

	notwendig	nicht notwendig
Have you seen the DVD which I bought yesterday?	☐	☐
The book that my sister gave me was boring.	☐	☐
Jill, whose parents are abroad at the moment, likes movies from the 60s.	☐	☐
That's the man who I saw in the bank.	☐	☐
This man, who loves detective stories, is my father.	☐	☐
I don't like the kind of cheese which you brought from the supermarket on Monday.	☐	☐
Mary's shop, which sells second-hand clothes, is open until 4 o'clock in the afternoon.	☐	☐

2 Setze in den folgenden Sätzen Kommas, wo diese erforderlich sind.

a) Our neighbour who knows much about butterflies is out for dinner.

b) This is the book that I have looked for for two hours now.

c) Will he meet John whose daughter's name is Joanne this afternoon?

d) Mrs Lombard who likes fast food won't come to the party.

e) The young lady who likes fast food won't come to the party.

f) Mr Armstrong who won the Tour de France several times lives in the States.

g) Her mother gave her the nice dress that she had bought in Paris.

h) The police officer wanted to talk to the man that he had seen in the bank two days ago.

i) The police officer wanted to talk to Mr Wayne who is a taxi driver.

Regeln: Relativpronomen

1. Ein Relativsatz beginnt meist mit einem sogenannten **Relativpronomen**, zum Beispiel mit *who, which, that* oder *whose*.
2. ***Who*** bezieht sich auf Personen.
   Which bezieht sich auf Dinge oder Tiere.
   Beispiele: *The girl who won the competition was very happy.*
   The car which I'd like to drive must be really fast.
   She has got a horse which is called San Salvador.
3. Das Relativpronomen ***that*** kann man sowohl für Personen als auch für Dinge und Tiere verwenden.
   Achtung: In nicht notwendigen Relativsätzen ist *that* unüblich!
   Beispiele: *Do you know the man that is talking to Toby?*
   This is the key that opens the back door.
   I've seen a camel that had lost its tail.
4. Das Relativpronomen ***whose*** (dessen, deren) kann bei Personen und Dingen verwendet werden.
   Beispiel: *The young boy whose bike was stolen is very unhappy.*

Tipp | Verwechsele *whose* nicht mit *who's* (wer ist)!

Übungen

3 *Who* oder *which*? Trage das richtige Relativpronomen ein.

a) This is Jerry, the cat ________ would like to be mouse.

b) These are the people ________ tried to catch Jerry.

c) This is the hole ___________ Jerry tried to hide in.

d) This is Sally ________ rescued (= *rettete*) Jerry.

e) And this is the milk ________ poor Jerry is going to drink now.

4 Streiche alle nicht erlaubten Relativpronomen der folgenden **notwendigen** Relativsätze durch.

a) The girl which/whose/that brother is fifteen likes playing tennis.

b) The letter that/who/which you sent me is two pages long.

c) She doesn't like the kind of music that/whose/who/which was played in the circus.

d) Everybody who/which/that knows how to sail a boat come here, please.

5 Streiche alle nicht erlaubten Relativpronomen der folgenden **nicht notwendigen** Relativsätze durch.

a) Our chemistry teacher, that/which/who is 35, will help you with the experiment.

b) Mr Bond gave his son a model airplane, that/whose/which he had bought in the toy shop.

c) Carol Woytyla, who/that/which was a bishop in Poland, became pope.

d) Yesterday I met Sue, that/which/who is always nice to talk to.

Tipp Benötigt ein Relativpronomen eine Präposition, dann wird diese meist nachgestellt.
Beispiele: *Bill is the boy Mr Carlson is proud of.*
This is exactly what I was looking for.

6 Übersetze mit nachgestellter Präposition.

a) Dies ist der Junge, vor dem Max Angst hat.

____

b) Wo ist (denn) das Buch, nach dem ich gerade suche?

____

c) Das ist der Mann, auf den jeder stolz ist.

____

Regeln: *Contact clauses*

1. In manchen Fällen darfst du das Relativpronomen weglassen. Solche Sätze heißen dann *contact clauses*. Relativpronomen können weggelassen werden, wenn sie als **Objekt** in einem **notwendigen** Relativsatz auftreten. Ob ein Relativpronomen ein Objekt ist, erkennst du daran, dass du mit „Wen/Wem oder was?“ nach ihm fragen kannst.
   Beispiele: *This man is the criminal who/that the detective has looked for since 1990.* (..., **den** der Kriminalbeamte seit 1990 gesucht hat.)
   Das Relativpronomen ist Objekt in einem notwendigen Relativsatz und kann daher weggelassen werden:
   → *This man is the criminal the detective has looked for since 1990.*
2. Achtung: In nicht notwendigen Relativsätzen gibt es keine *contact clauses*, d.h. das Relativpronomen darf nicht weggelassen werden!

Übung

7 Streiche das Relativpronomen in den Sätzen durch, in denen es weggelassen werden kann.

a) John Pearl is the magician <u>who</u> knows how to turn teachers into frogs.

b) The car <u>which</u> we rented in Scotland was brandnew.

c) The man <u>that</u> she was talking to is the chief executive of MM Toys.

d) The company <u>which</u> I work for was founded 10 years ago.

e) Does he know the person <u>that</u> wrote a letter of application to him?

f) Look at the dog <u>which</u> is sitting on the roof!

g) Have you ever met someone <u>who</u> really liked school?

h) Here's the magazine <u>that</u> you wanted to read.

Fehler-Check

Setze, wo nötig, ein passendes Relativpronomen ein.

London is one of the most beautiful cities _________ the world has ever seen. London has got many famous museums and tourist attractions _________ are known all over the world. The Tower Bridge, _________ is the most famous bridge in London, is visited by millions of tourist every year. The history of London, _________ is going back to its founding by the Romans, _________ called it Londinium, is most interesting. London is a city _________ is the world's largest financial centre alongside New York. The Underground, _________ is the oldest underground railway network in the world, is the second largest in the world after Shanghai. Greater London, _________ covers an area of 1600 square kilometers, has a population of about 7.5 million. The River Thames is a tidal river _________ makes London vulnerable to flooding. In 1974 people started a project _________ will help to make the city safer – the Thames Barrier. It will hold back water _________ might run into London in periods of heavy rainfall.

☐ Punkte	9–11 Punkte	5–8 Punkte	weniger als 5 Punkte
	Super!	In Ordnung!	Bitte noch einmal üben!

To-infinitives – Sätze richtig vereinfachen

It's a rainy Sunday morning. Mike doesn't know what he shall do. It's too boring if he just sits on the sofa and watches TV. He knows how he can play the piano, but he doesn't like to, because he played it for four hours yesterday. Poor Mike. It's absolutely terrible him to see in such a bad mood.

Regeln

Der *to*-Infinitiv (*to* + Grundform) ist eine Möglichkeit, Sätze im Englischen zu vereinfachen.
Er kann nach folgenden Wortarten stehen:

- nach Fragewörtern:
  She doesn't know where to go. (Sie weiß nicht, wohin sie gehen soll.)
  He asked me how to get to the station. (Er fragte mich, wie er zum Bahnhof komme.)
- nach Adjektiven:
  This question is easy to answer. (Diese Frage kann leicht beantwortet werden.)
  It's interesting to get to know more about reptiles. (Es ist interessant, mehr über Reptilien zu erfahren.)
- nach Nomen:
  It was a great idea to go to the zoo. (Es war eine großartige Idee, in den Zoo zu gehen.)
  He told her about his decision to go to France. (Er erzählte ihr von seiner Entscheidung, nach Frankreich zu gehen.)

Übungen

1 Verbessere den Klassenarbeitsauszug. Schreibe in dein Heft.

2 Übersetze die folgenden Sätze. Verwende *to*-Infinitive.

a) Ich weiß nicht, wie ich dieses Problem lösen soll.

b) Hat er sie gefragt, wann er mit der Arbeit beginnen soll?

c) Schön, Sie zu treffen.

d) Es war eine große Überraschung, meinen Bruder zu sehen.

e) Weißt du, wie man diese Datei (= *file*) öffnet?

f) Es war schrecklich, das Schiff sinken zu sehen.

g) Diese Wand zu streichen, war eine gute Idee.

h) Es ist ein hohes Risiko, diesen Berg im Winter zu besteigen.

i) Frag ihn, wie du ihm helfen kannst.

Tipp Verwende den *to*-Infinitiv auch nach den Verben *want, would like, would love, would prefer.*
Beispiel: *Elisa wants to join the judo club, but her father would like to talk to the coach first.*

3 Vereinfache die folgenden Sätze, indem du *to*-Infinitive verwendest.

a) She didn't know what she should answer.

____

b) I asked him where I could go.

____

c) I was surprised when I saw Aunt Olivia with her oldtimer car. ______________

____

____

____

d) It was rather difficult when I had to solve the problem so quickly.

____

____

e) Can you tell me how I can loosen this screw?

____

f) I told him where he had to go to get a new passport.

____

Fehler-Check

Trage die fehlenden Wörter ein.

9 o'clock. It's difficult __________ so early in the morning. I would prefer __________ in bed all day, but it's not __________ to explain this idea to my mother. On the other hand, it's just boring ________ lie in bed and do nothing. I don't know __________ to do now. Perhaps it might be a great ________ to go to the zoo this Saturday morning, but I __________ how to get there, because the busses aren't running today. They're on strike. It's really terrible __________ without a vehicle. My brother's bike is easy ________ ride, but he's away on a sports camp this weekend. I would like __________ my own bike, but it's difficult to ________ one, if you don't have the __________ to buy one. I must ask Pete where ________ cheap used bikes. Perhaps he ________ how to get one. It might be a good plan ________ go to the sports club today. I would love my mother ________ take me there, but I think she would prefer to __________ in her armchair and read a book. Let's see ________ I can persuade her ________ give me a lift. Oh, it's a nuisance __________ spend a boring Saturday's morning if you don't know __________ to do!

☐ **Punkte**

17–21 Punkte Super!

10–16 Punkte In Ordnung!

weniger als 10 Punkte Bitte noch einmal üben!

Lösungen

L

Kapitel 1: Grundlegende Fehler – leicht vermeidbar!

Fehlerquelle Pronomen

Seite 6

1
a) Can you hear me?
b) Can you help me?
c) I love you.
d) I believe you.
e) You often meet him.
f) Tell him the story.
g) Does he like her?
h) Trust (in) her.
i) They often visit us (see us).
j) They give us money.
k) I need you.
l) He'll soon write you.

Seite 7

2
a) Can you hear me, Lucy? – Yes, I can, but I can't see you.
b) Mike is fourteen, he's not twelve. His sister's twelve and she's as bold as brass.
c) Don't touch him, Susan. He's in a bad mood.
d) We don't know how to solve this problem. So can you please give us some advice.
e) Don't tell me lies, my son. I know that you always try to find excuses.
f) Come on, give them a new chance. They have never disappointed us/you so far.

3 Hello, my name's Percy. [...] We live under the root of an old [...]. They say they can't afford a better [...]. So their dream of a bigger house [...]. I don't blame them for [...]. It simply is their money. Curly, my brother, left us two months ago [...] as a magician at his aunt's [...].

Fehler-Check

Seite 8

1. Mary, why don't you want to come to my birthday party? All my friends except you will be there.
2. You must call me this afternoon. I need some advice.
3. Have you seen my new bike, Gilbert? Isn't it wonderful?
4. Why doesn't your sister like me, Daisy? I like her.
5. One day, when Oliver and his friends came home, they saw her, a beauty, a princess!
6. Thomas A. Edison was born in his grandfather's house in 1847.
7. You must see the Millers, Hannah. Please meet them at Trafalgar Square.
8. I don't like those people. They don't really see my problem.
9. You're really kind, Mr Benson. But can you help me one more time?
10. Ssh – the kids are sleeping. They had a hard day.
11. Why don't you call the police, Victor? They can help you.

12. Excuse me, can you please show me the way to the station?
13. Go to Marta's father. He is a dentist. And he's a good one.
14. I know, you don't believe me, Jo. But I'm telling the truth.

***He, she, it* – das -s muss mit**

Seite 9

1 Tom collects posters. He likes pop posters best. Pop posters, he thinks, are the most wonderful of all posters. Whenever there is a pop concert in his town, he wants to get one of the posters fixed to the boards in the streets. Sometimes he asks for a poster at the tourist office and he can usually have one. Very often, his friends, who know that he is interested in pop posters, give him a nice new poster as a birthday present. His father knows about his son's hobby, so when his colleagues' children go to a pop event, he always says: "Don't forget to look for posters!"

Seite 10

2 a) Susan never goes to school by bus, she walks.
b) My younger sister often cries when she's alone at home.
c) Max often switches on the lights in his room in the afternoon.
d) Her daughter usually does her homework in the kitchen.
e) He pays a lot for his mobile phone calls every month.
f) Fred attends a language course abroad, so he misses his family.

Seite 11

3 a) Ken might know much more about the secret.
b) Charlotte wants to spend her summer holiday in Scotland.
c) His sister must do her homework in her room.
d) She never goes to church on Sundays.

Seite 12

4 a) Does Sally's brother live in New York City?
b) My father doesn't (will not) invite his friends to his birthday party.
c) Does this wardrobe really fit into my parents' bedroom?

Seite 13

5 He look likes → He looks like; he don't like → he doesn't like; He know much → He knows much; he can't speaks → he can't speak; He often gos → He often goes; he never talk → he never talks; he buies hundreds → he buys hundreds; he never pay → he never pays; to gets married → to get married; he doesn't likes → he doesn't like; He dream → He dreams; he must cries → he must cry; He can't sees → He can't see; he don't wear → he doesn't wear; He musts work → He must work; he doesn't goes → he doesn't go; He feel sick → He feels sick; he never see → he never sees; He often rushs → He often rushes; but his never late

→ but he's never late; He can't carries → He can't carry; he doesn't wants → he doesn't want; He don't smile → He doesn't smile; he tell us → he tells us; He doesn't talks → He doesn't talk; he never finish → he never finishes; Everyone know → Everyone knows

Fehler-Check

Seite 14

Pete's big problem

Once a year in summer Pete must travel to his aunt in New York City. He loves America, but he doesn't like going on a plane. Although so many planes fly across the Atlantic Ocean every day, he doesn't understand why only few people are afraid of flying. When asked for the reason for this, he can't give a good answer. He often goes to the airport and watches the jets, but he hates the idea of being on one of them. Does he know how safe flying on a plane really is? At least it seems to be safer than going by car. His uncle, who works as a pilot, always says: "The most dangerous part of an air travel is the lift to the airport in a taxi!" He likes giving this statement.

Word order – Ordnung im Satz

Seite 16

1 a) She saw him in Brooklyn last Wednesday.
b) Sue heard a strange noise on the playground yesterday.
c) David did not answer that question that day.
d) Did you take many pictures at your party last week?

2 a) Did you really give me the money yesterday?
b) I sent the book back to him, but he never got it.
c) Mr Benson teaches me Latin.
d) Have you written him a lot of letters?/Did you write ...?
e) May/Can I tell you a joke?

Seite 17

3 a) Tom never writes letters.
b) My mum sometimes takes the bus to Soho.
c) He's often seen a ghost in his room.
d) My aunt has always been a gossip girl.

Fehler-Check

Seite 18

1. I would like to ask you a question, Dad.
2. Alan, I met your girlfriend in Bath last week.
3. Do you really play tennis in Greenwich every day, Isabella?

Lösungen

4. I often stay in school in the afternoons.
5. Could you please bring me a cup of tea, Sir?
6. I don't like the fog in San Francisco.
7. How many books have you given to your brother at Christmas, Priscilla?
8. Tell me the truth, Pete.

There is ..., there are ..., this, that, these, those

Seite 19

1 a) Are there many German immigrants in Australia?
b) Is there much money on your bank account, Lily?
c) My God, there's so much rain in Scotland.
d) There are twenty pupils (sitting) in the bus.

Seite 20

2 There's a monkey in the tree.
There are three fish in the aquarium.
There are two tigers in the cage.
There's a giraffe behind the kiosk.
There are two zebras on the grass.
There's a dolphin in the pool.

Seite 21

3 a) This bike here came from the right.
b) That green car over there didn't stop.
c) Those two joggers over there couldn't see the accident.
d) These wheel traces here are of another car.
e) This woman here saw everything.

Seite 22

Fehler-Check

Good morning, this is Julia Sullivan reporting from this year's tennis cup final in Southampton. There are already hundreds of spectators sitting on those upper seats over there opposite to me. They are waiting for the players to come and start this important match. There isn't much time left, so the match will start in a couple of minutes. There's a strange murmur in the stadium because you can see those dark, grey clouds approaching from the west. Will this match be started, or must all people find shelter from the rain in one of those shelter huts over there?
Oh, my God, what's this? There's a first thunderbolt! Look, all those people over there are running down to the entrance gates. They don't want to be struck by lightning, they want to leave this terrible scene! And it's becoming foggy. I can see this monitor in front of me, but I can't see those people in the next row not

far away. What a disaster! And right now it starts raining. I don't like this weather. There are so many people, and they all want to go home now. There's nowhere to stay because all these people are nervously pacing around.

S-Genitiv oder of-Genitiv?

Seite 24

1. richtig: b), d), e), f), h), j)
   falsch: a) (her uncle's wife), c) (my sister's suitcases), g) (Donald Duck's nephews), i) (Lydia's dream), k) (the name of this street)

2. a) my brother's book
   b) the title of this story
   c) the Miller family's problem
   d) the children's questions
   e) the trees in the Clarks' garden
   f) Fred's secret/mystery
   g) these people's bikes
   h) the colour of this flower

Seite 25

3. a) I like my nephew's two dogs.
   b) Our parents' new house is quite big.
   c) I know the title of this book.
   d) These people's clothes are wet.

4. a) The Irvings'/~~Irving's~~/~~Irvings~~ model railway was rather expensive.
   b) I don't like the colours in ~~Cathys~~/~~Cathies~~/Cathy's new room.
   c) The ~~Cavendishs~~/~~Cavendish's~~/Cavendishes' garage is painted blue.
   d) ~~Dennis~~/Dennis's kindergarten class is called 'The Rugby Fighters'.

Fehler-Check

Seite 26

Hi, Steven,

You want to know something about my brother's stay in New York City? Here you are. The name of the school is Southpark High. Some months ago my parents' plan was to fly over to New York to see if everything's alright. I'm sure they wanted to see the home of the host family/the host family's home and the surroundings of this interesting city. In a letter, however, my brother wrote about his friends' plans of taking him along on a trip to Chicago. To be honest, I think it was my brother's idea to keep my parents away with this letter. He doesn't want to have them with him in New York because he's got a girlfriend there, called Paris. Paris's parents live in the most expensive borough of New York. Her relatives' homes are in the heart of Manhattan. I must end now, because I have to go to the doctor's. I sprained the ankle of my left foot in a basketball match yesterday.

Lösungen

Articles – bestimmt oder unbestimmt?

Seite 28

1 a) an expensive pencil
b) the wonderful beaches
c) a fantastic view
d) an old bear
e) the best hotel

2 I'm packing my bags, because I'm going to fly to Venice soon. In my big suitcase I've got a green shirt, an extra pair of shoes, a woolen coat, -- orange braces, a pair of brown trousers, an old-fashioned hat, -- grey slippers and an old teddy bear.

3 a) a universal truth
b) an olive scarf
c) a United Airlines flight
d) an audiovisual show
e) an Indian meal
f) a university
g) an angry man
h) an idea

Seite 29

4 a) Silence is golden
b) The silence of the hammers
c) The life of (the) heart
d) Face life!
e) Love can heal
f) The love of his life

Seite 30

Fehler-Check

a) After -- dinner, he went down to a (wenn mehrere in der Straße vorhanden), the (wenn nur eine vorhanden) discotheque in -- Boston Road, where he met a beautiful girl – the very love of his life. -- Life was back!
b) Oh, good heavens, are you really the man I got married to in the Alps in -- December?
c) An/The old lady told her she saw her play the violin years ago on -- TV.
d) I like -- literature in general, but I don't like the literature of the 90s.
e) The orange/-- Orange shirts hung on an old rotten line in -- Bond Street.
f) "I was always late for -- lunch at -- school," he said on the radio.
g) The Pacific Ocean is the biggest of all oceans.
h) A United Nations commission decided on the problem of poverty in -- Africa.
i) -- Money is not too important in -- life!
j) Are you really telling me that the money I gave you on -- Monday is gone?

Have got oder *have*?

Seite 31

1 a) She has terrible problems.
b) You have got ten minutes (time).
c) The Millers have three cars.
d) Pete has got two sisters.

❷ a) She's got two bikes and brandnew rollerskates. Seite 32
b) My mother's got three sisters.
c) They've got so many books in their living-room.
d) I've got a big, big problem.
e) We've got a lot of uncles and aunts.

❸ a) Doesn't he have two sisters? – Yes, he does. Seite 33
b) The Prestons haven't got a new garage.
c) Didn't you have any answer to this question?
d) I don't have any idea.
e) I haven't got any idea.
f) Do they have a new car? – Yes, they do.
g) Have you got a pencil? – Yes, I have.
h) She has got two horses.

❹ My friend Anatomus is an alien from a planet in the Andromeda system. He hasn't got two but three eyes. He has (oder: has got) four tentacles and green skin. He doesn't have any legs. He's got two big wheels to move on and he's got red long hair. Has he got a nose? No, he's got two of them! Does he have a face? Of course, he's got the most wonderful face in the universe and the best smile!

Fehler-Check Seite 34

a) Has Lynn got a nice room? – No, she hasn't. It's far too small.
b) Do your parents have trouble with your younger sister? – Yes, they do. My sister has got a lot of problems at the moment.
c) Sue: I really don't have too much time, so hurry up, please.
Ann: Have you got more time tomorrow? Sue: I'm afraid, I haven't.
d) She doesn't have/hasn't got a brother, but she has ('s) got two more sisters.
e) Have you got some tools? – Tools? – Yes, I mean, do you have a hammer, a screwdriver and a knife? – Yes, I do.
f) Has Mary got a headache? – No, she hasn't.
g) My uncle has got a big family. Does he have twins? – No, he doesn't. He's got three girls, two boys and four dogs.
h) Does Sue have her exercise-books at home? – Yes, she does.
i) My aunt's got blue earrings.
j) I don't have/haven't got much pocket money a week. How much do you have?
k) Hey, do you have my pen? – No, I don't. I've got my own.
l) He has never got much time. He's always hurrying.

L

Lösungen

False friends

Seite 37

1 Dear Olivia,

How are you? Imagine, I got my new notebook yesterday. I waited all day, and finally, late in the afternoon, my father handed me over a letter from the headmaster of our school. It said that I had been well-behaved in class, so there wasn't any reason for having an extra lesson every week. My father congratulated on this good news saying: "I haven't got a new mobile/cell phone for you, but this notebook here will be yours, because I'm very happy you improved at school." So my father's really got a better opinion of me.

2 a) Tim is a well-behaved child, he never drinks his sister's coffee.
b) I think we should paint the bedroom yellow. What's your opinion?
c) My skin is very sensitive.
d) We thought our dog had swallowed some poison. He was very quiet.
e) This strawberry jam is great!
f) She is a very sensitive and quiet person.
g) My father's advice is often handy.

3 a) A brave, but sensitive rat wanted to spend the holidays in a quiet café.
b) A well-behaved boy wrote a letter about a noodle recipe.

Seite 38

Fehler-Check

a) Dr Hudson gave me a prescription against my terrible headache. He was of the opinion that I have caught a heavy cold.
b) This recipe is from my grandma.
c) He has bought nice gifts for all his family.
d) What would you like for breakfast? – I would like to have a cup of coffee, bread and butter and some orange marmalade.
e) Oh, the battery's run down. Can I please use your mobile/cell phone to call my mum? – Yes, you can, but you're still on time to get home.
f) Did you get a new skateboard? – Yes, I did. My father gave me a blue one some days before he became the headmaster of Lincoln School.
g) May I give you some advice? Take an umbrella. It's going to rain.
h) Excuse me, the reason why I am late is: I couldn't find my mobile/cell phone.

Kapitel 2: Fehlerquellen rund ums Nomen

Plurals – regelmäßig oder unregelmäßig?

Seite 40

1 four trees; two cars; three tables; three eggs; two pianos; five bottles

2
a) I know all the countries in the world.
b) He ate half a kilo of cherries.
c) Are the kids still at school?
d) She must prepare for the test within five days.
e) My two bosses are on holiday at the moment.
f) Our house has got twelve windows.
g) This is one of the most beautiful bays in England.
h) Do you know these red berries over there?
i) There are so many rivers in Scotland.
j) Oh, look at these beautiful watches.

Seite 42

3 On this photo I can see three geese, five women, two children, four shelves, a sheep, six men, nine oxen, eight knives, two mice, ten teeth, three calves and two feet.

Fehler-Check

a) I got ten ~~kisss~~ on my cheek from my little cousin Edward.	kisses
b) Mr Spearmint, the dentist, said: "Your ~~toothes~~ are okay."	teeth
c) Look, the ~~lorrys~~ are being loaded with tons of sand.	lorries
d) Last night I dreamt of three ~~mens~~ and two ~~womens~~. They had	men; women
really big ~~foots~~. They were talking to their four ~~childs~~ and	feet; children
playing with six ~~gooses~~ and two sheep.	geese
e) He doesn't want to watch the finals on TV. He likes being in the	
stadium to see the ~~matchs~~ live.	matches
f) The ~~boies~~ and girls were quietly sitting on their ~~chaires~~.	boys; chairs
g) She knows the capitals of most ~~countrys~~.	countries
h) Please put the books on the ~~shelfs~~.	shelves
i) On his voyage Paul sailed into four different ~~baies~~.	bays
j) Four ~~eys~~ can see more than only two.	eyes
k) Don't forget to brush your ~~teeths~~.	teeth
l) Our ~~childs'~~ new dog is called Alexander the Great.	children's
m) So many ~~peoples~~ have died in the plane crash.	people

L

Lösungen

Mengenangaben: *some* oder *any*, *much* oder *many*?

Seite 44

1 a) I'm sorry, there isn't any coffee left. You must take some tea.
b) He had some quick answers, but they didn't make any sense.
c) Teacher: Are there any questions? No? Then let's do some work.
d) Sophie hasn't got any money left.

2 a) There's no excuse for this behaviour.
b) There isn't any excuse for this behaviour.
c) Can I have some cheese?
d) Is there any cheese?
e) I know some of the boys from Boston.
f) I don't know any of the boys from Boston.
g) Would you like to have some jam?
h) I've no idea.
i) I haven't got any idea. Oder: I don't have any idea.

Seite 45

3 viel Spaß: much fun; viele Menschen: many people; viel Geld: much money; viele Tiere: many animals; viele Wörter: many words; viel Liebe: much love; viel Sand: much sand; viele Lineale: many rulers

4 four oranges, two bottles of milk, a (one) kilo of butter, two bars of chocolate, one litre of apple juice, four packs of rice

5 Lemon and potato cake
Heat 225 grams of butter in a cake tin. Cream the butter and half a kilo of sugar in a bowl. Whisk in some potatoes. Crack in some eggs. Don't use too many of them. Mix half a kilo of flour with one teaspoon of baking powder and put it in the bowl with the sugar. Any further instructions cannot be given because I don't know how to finish the cake. Better ask some of your friends.

Seite 46

Fehler-Check

a) Don't eat too many/much/any chocolate.
b) Have you got much/any/no idea how to translate this sentence?
c) A lot of/Any/Much people think ice-hockey is a brutal sport.
d) How much/any/many/a lot of roads must a man walk down ...
e) I'd like to have a cup --/of/some tea, please.
f) There's much/any/no way out!
g) Can I have some/any mustard, please?

h) This really doesn't make many/a lot of/no/any sense.
i) Steven hasn't got a lot of/much/no/any pets. He's only got a rabbit.
j) There's too many/any/a lot of/much water in the pot.
k) In my pencil-case I've got many/much pencils and much/some rulers.
l) I don't understand. Can you please give me a lot of/some/no advice?
m) Any/No/Some dogs are really aggressive.
n) A sportscar is any/no/a lot of/much faster than a limousine.
o) Pooh, there isn't many/no/any salt in this soup. How awful!
p) I've been to much/no/many countries in Europe, but the country I like very many/any/some/much is Switzerland.
q) Can't you see that there is too many/some/much milk in the cup?

Kapitel 3: Zeitformen *(tenses)* richtig gebrauchen

Simple present oder *present progressive*?

1 a) Paula goes to church on Sundays twice a month. Seite 48
b) Don' forget your raincoat. It rains a lot on the British Isles.
c) Most people know/think that having a big car is too expensive.
d) Most cats don't like dogs.

2 a) Five times eight is 40. / Five multiplied by eight is 40.
b) The sun goes down/sets in the west.
c) If you heat ice, it melts.
d) Plants produce oxygen.
e) Children need love.

3 a) She is buying some coffee at the supermarket. Seite 50
b) They are spending their holidays without us this week.
c) Are you sleeping?

4 a) Oh no, look, this young boy is having a beer!
b) The film was good. All the people are clapping their hands.
c) Shh, can you hear this? My brother is snoring.
d) Oh no! She's really sitting next to her English teacher.

5 a) The sun is shining, so it isn't raining. Seite 51
b) Four children are standing in front of the school entrance door.

Lösungen

c) Three boys are building a snowman.
d) A girl is throwing a snowball.
e) Two boys are fighting on the ground.
f) A teacher is running towards the girl.
g) The school bell is ringing.
h) A boy is climbing (on) a tree.

Seite 52

Fehler-Check

Every Monday evening Joe tries to improve his judo skills in the gym. He loves this kind of sport because he thinks it really supports his discipline and his fitness. He usually starts his training with fifty sit-ups. Today, however, things are different. Right now he is sitting in the changing room, because he can't concentrate. He is dreaming about this wonderful young girl. He often dreams about girls, although he never addresses them at school. But this very moment he is floating on cloud nine, because his heart is beating fast and a warm feeling is running through his body. Normally he never loses control. This evening, however, his head is like a beehouse. Angels are singing wonderful, spheric songs, and magical odours are passing by his nose, although he rarely cares about perfumes. But what on earth is this? Two strong hands are shaking his shoulder, and a loud voice is hammering into his ears. "Hey, are you sleeping? Wake up! It's time to get to the gym."

Simple past oder *past progressive*?

Seite 54

1
a) played	b) answered	c) laughed	d) turned	e) talked
f) needed	g) waited	h) shouted	i) liked	j) helped
k) cried	l) came	m) drove	n) found	o) had
p) made	q) ran	r) shut	s) slept	t) stood
u) thought	v) wore			

Seite 55

2
a) I had a headache.
b) She was twelve.
c) They spoke Spanish.
d) Freddy knew her.
e) We liked baseball.
f) She had breakfast early.
g) It rained.
h) They laughed a lot.

Seite 56

3
a) The two girls didn't reach the exit.
b) The old lady wasn't excited.
c) She didn't have a wonderful view of London.
d) They didn't drink much.

4 a) Did the two girls reach the exit?
b) Was the old lady excited?
c) Did she have a wonderful view of London?
d) Did they drink much?

Seite 57

5 a) The old man was having a beer, when suddenly a dog started to bark.
b) First, I finished my homework, then I went out.
c) When I woke up in the night, I heard that my brother was snoring.
d) She was writing a letter when there was a knock on the door.
e) He was tidying up his room, when suddenly there was a scream.
f) When they went to bed last night, the birds weren't singing.

Fehler-Check

Seite 58

After the summer holidays Mr Roman, the English teacher, asked the pupils to write a short summary on their holiday activities. Sue wrote: "In the first week my brother and I took part in a summer camp in Wales. On the first day we went to a small village and visited a Roman theatre. The next day we were going by bus to a nice lake when we suddenly heard a strange noise. The bus stopped and the bus driver told us that he couldn't go on with us. So we had to walk the rest of the distance to our camp. The next day we tried to cross a river on a raft. While we were paddling, Tom fell into the water. We tore him out of the water while he was crying all the time. On our last day we were trailing down a lonesome path, when we saw Bill, one of the boys, sitting in a tree. A barking dog stood/was standing under it. First it pulled open the boy's rucksack and then it ate his lunch."

***Present perfect* oder *simple past*?**

Seite 60

1

	simple past	*present perfect*
I – live – here	I lived here.	I have lived here.
it – rain	It rained.	It has rained.
she – see – me	She saw me.	She has seen me.
he – know – her	He knew her.	He has known her.
we – be – there	We were there.	We have been there.
you – have – tea	You had tea.	You have had tea.

Lösungen

Seite 61

2 a) She has been to New York very often. So she has seen the Statue of Liberty many times in her life.

b) Our teacher has shown us many films about US national parks this year. Unfortunately, I didn't see/haven't seen all of them because I was ill for some weeks.

c) Where have you been, Tom?

d) What have you done, Susan?

e) Has she read the book?

f) Sarah can't come. She has broken her leg.

g) Look! John has given me his iPod.

Seite 62

3 Mary has waited for Tom for three hours. She hasn't seen him for years, so she's extremely excited. Since 2008, when they met for the first time in Rome, they haven't had any contact. Oh, there he is! Look at him, he hasn't changed. He looks like the young boy Mary has been in love with from the first moment they saw each other.

4 a) Much has changed since I lived here as a boy.

b) She has been unemployed for two years.

c) Since 2005 my father has been a member of the volleyball club. Two years ago he became president.

d) Our house has become quiet since he travelled to Boston last month.

e) Look, it has rained.

f) Who has drunk my coffee?

g) Tom wrote a letter to Mary last Tuesday, but she hasn't got it.

h) In my childhood I often saw big animals in the zoo. But I have never seen a bear as big as this one.

i) Who has done it?

Seite 64

Fehler-Check

a) won

b) have you written

c) Has he read

d) did you eat

e) met; haven't slept

f) have fought; have not been

g) hasn't arrived

h) went; haven't seen; has often been

i) bought; have bought

j) Has he told; did he do

k) have you had

l) has talked

Irregular verbs – richtig verwendet

Seite 66

1

Infinitiv	*past-tense*-Form	Perfekt-Form	deutsch
tell	told	told	sagen, erzählen
run	ran	run	rennen
steal	stole	stolen	stehlen
make	made	made	machen
get	got	got	erhalten, bekommen
catch	caught	caught	fangen
swim	swam	swum	schwimmen
fight	fought	fought	kämpfen
know	knew	known	wissen, kennen
bring	brought	brought	bringen
read	read	read	lesen
teach	taught	taught	unterrichten
write	wrote	written	schreiben
take	took	taken	nehmen
keep	kept	kept	behalten, aufheben
drive	drove	driven	fahren

Seite 67

2
a) Lara went to New Zealand two weeks ago.
b) Have you ever eaten a plumcake?
c) Last month Pete met his mother in Los Angeles.
d) She hasn't bought a new scarf so far. She still uses her old one.
e) No, I didn't lose my MP3-Player on Wednesday. I have never lost anything in my life.
f) You can easily translate this German movie title into English. „Die vergessene Welt" in English is "The Forgotten World".
g) She caught the ball with one hand.
h) Yesterday I swam in the lake.
i) When he saw that the police were coming in his direction he quickly ran away.
j) While she was working as an au pair in Washington she kept in touch with her family via Skype.

Fehler-Check

Seite 68

a) Although she was very exhausted after the concert, the pop star gave an interview and answered all the questions.
b) Did they really sell their house last year?

Lösungen

c) Picasso made this painting shortly before he died.
d) Has your team ever beaten our team?
e) Where's my pencil-case? Somebody has stolen it!
f) He doesn't teach Latin, but he has taught Maths for years, and he has been quite a good teacher.
g) My aunt always knows/knew how to tell a good joke.
h) I've waited for you since 9 o'clock. Where have you been?
i) Tell me what she said yesterday.
j) We didn't know much about the Italian language, so we fetched a German-Italian dictionary.
k) He was 16 when he met her for the first time.

Going to future oder *will future*?

Seite 70

1
a) Take an umbrella. It's going to rain.
b) The plane is rolling to the runway. It's going to take off.
c) She's bought a ticket at the counter. She's going to take the bus to Memphis.

2
a) Is he going to have driving lessons?
b) Is she going to have a baby next month?
c) Are you going to pack your suitcase?
d) Are they going to leave the country in an hour?
e) Am I going to get my hair cut?

Seite 71

3
a) She thinks (that) her host mother will be strict.
b) Maybe she won't like her room.
c) She will probably have problems with the language.
d) She's sure that she will like the children.
e) Perhaps she will hate the American food.

Seite 72

Fehler-Check

a) I think the team will win next Saturday.
b) Oh, I've dropped the matches. – No problem, I will get you new ones.
c) She's pregnant. She will have her baby in April.
d) The sun will set at 6.30 tomorrow. But we are not going to watch the sunset, because the weather forecast is horrible.
e) Pete is worried about his English test. Will he succeed?
f) Watch out, this firecracker is going to explode!

g) My grandpa will be 70 next week. That's why we are going to have a big family party on Sunday. What will the weather be like? 'High Edmund' is approaching from the Atlantic. There will be sunshine.
h) Next Monday will be May 1st. So there will be a holiday.
i) Are you going to spend your next holiday in Ireland?
j) What would you like to have for dinner? – I think I will take a soup first.
k) She's sure that her brother will be back soon.

Kapitel 4: Fehlerquelle Adjektiv und Adverb

Adjektive richtig steigern und vergleichen

1 a) P b) S c) K d) K e) S f) K g) S h) P i) K j) K Seite 74

2

Positiv	Komparativ	Superlativ
short	shorter	shortest
industrious (fleißig)	more industrious	most industrious
curly	curlier	curliest
interesting	more interesting	most interesting
noisy	noisier	noisiest
noble	nobler	noblest
hip	hipper	hippest

3 a) This is the most expensive newspaper. Seite 75
b) Are you as old as my brother, Ella?
c) You are the dullest/most stupid boy on earth.

Fehler-Check Seite 76

My house is bigger than my neighbour's. I'm sure my house is the biggest building in our street. Although my sports car is not as fast as John's, it is the fastest car I've ever had. To be honest, it's even more expensive than a Ferrarri. I'm really not a stupid blowhard, but the worst thing you can do is give people the idea that they are better than you. That's why I always wear the coolest clothes I can get. Sometimes I also love good fast food, but what I think is the greatest feeling, is going out for fine dinners in the most famous restaurant in town. I'm a bit shy sometimes, although I have paid a lot of money to my psychiatrist, who, by the way, is one of the best in our country. In my last session with him, I asked him why I haven't found a nice girl so far. He just said: "Tom, you are the nicest man on earth!"

L

Lösungen

Adverbien richtig platzieren

Seite 77

1 a) Jan often works until late at night.
b) She has never been in Paris.
c) We sometimes go to the zoo late in the afternoon.
d) He's always excited before tests.
e) They regularly help their father in the garden.

Seite 78

2 horrible → horribly; silly → in a silly way/manner; extreme → extremely; mad → madly; friendly → in a friendly way/manner; easy → easily; quiet → quietly; good → well

Seite 79

3 Last Tuesday Jimmy had his first/~~firstly~~ French test at school. When he entered his classroom he was calm/~~calmly~~. But when he got his paper, he started to laugh ~~furious~~/furiously. His teacher said: "You have to be ~~absolute~~/absolutely quiet/~~quietly~~, Jimmy! Listen, all the others are working ~~quiet~~/quietly. They can't concentrate ~~proper~~/properly." But Jimmy couldn't stop laughing, so he left the room ~~quick~~/quickly.

4 a) My cat Tabby was hungrily eating her food.
b) Leon, the lion, was lazily sitting on the sofa.
c) Maxwell, my chameleon, was patiently looking at me.
d) Homer, the bulldog, was hastily running into the kitchen.
e) Cleopatra, the spider was happily watching 'Spiderman' in the living-room until midnight.
f) Ramses, the dromedary, was nervously waiting in the bathroom.

Seite 80

5 a) Mary was reading the newspaper in the dining-room until late in the morning.
b) When she came into the chapel she saw a statue in the centre of a pool.
c) At midnight something dark came through the garden gate.
Oder: Something dark came through the garden gate at midnight.
d) He often met his friend in the churchyard at 10 o'clock on Sundays.
e) Mary-Lou slowly drove home from the snackbar last Monday.

Seite 81

6 a) Every summer many people travel to the coasts in Great Britain.
b) They often visit the wonderful old churches in the villages in the east.
c) They sometimes (Sometimes they) go shopping in the shops in the main street until late in the evening.
d) There you can always find many souvenirs on the shelves.

Fehler-Check

Seite 82

a) I haven't been in Britain for ages.
b) He quickly answered the question.
c) He answered the question angrily.
d) They're often late for work.
e) Tom really behaves stupidly at the moment.
f) My father sometimes likes going for a walk.
g) Have you ever been to London?
h) She's got twenty cats in her house in Brighton.
i) Mrs Thomson often cleans all the windows.
j) They cared about his little dog in a lovely way.

Kapitel 5: Satzkonstruktionen: systematisch richtig!

Imperatives und *modal auxiliaries*

Seite 83

1 a) Don't write into your book!
b) Take your finger out of your mouth!
c) Open the window!
d) Don't get on my nerves!
e) Don't stand around, work!

Seite 85

2 You can have this novel and you can read the first twenty pages today. You needn't pay (anything) for it. But you must put the book on the shelf in the evening.

3 a) My sister can't swim. She has never been taught how to swim.
b) Can you help me, please? I can't finish this puzzle without you.
c) Must I really lay the table? – No, you needn't.
d) Pupils mustn't be in their classroom during breaks.
e) You needn't tell me, I already know the story.
f) Oh, it's late, I have to go home now.
g) You don't have to help me. I will get along without you.

Fehler-Check

Seite 86

Richtig sind: a, c, d, e, f, g, j, l, m

Conditional sentences

Seite 88

1 a) If you don't do this exercise, you won't pass the test.
b) You won't be hungry this evening if you eat so much chocolate.

Lösungen

c) If you don't stop phoning, I will tear the plug.

d) If you are that nervous in the test, you will make a lot of mistakes.

e) You will miss the film if you don't hurry.

Seite 88

2 Hier sind verschiedene Lösungen möglich. Wichtig ist, dass du die richtigen Zeitformen verwendet hast.

a) If they travel to Paris in summer, they will see the Eiffel Tower.

b) She will be very angry if he doesn't tell her the secret.

c) If he doesn't get an answer, he will become impatient.

d) Mr Miller won't buy the car if the seller doesn't reduce its price.

Seite 89

3 a) If you told me the secret, I wouldn't tell anybody.

b) I would find the treasure if you gave me the map.

c) If I found the gold, I would give you half of it.

d) If I had my gold, I wouldn't get on your nerves any longer.

e) I would buy a new play station if I got much money for my gold.

f) I wouldn't go to school any longer if I was/were rich.

Seite 90

Fehler-Check

a) If Tim joined our team, we would win the next match.

b) Tina will be able to go shopping with us later if she does her homework now.

c) If you lose your passport, you will have to go to the police.

d) If she loved me, she would tell me.

e) We would buy a house if we had 300 000 €.

f) If Mary saved more money, she could go to the concert.

g) If he knew the effects of alcoholism, he wouldn't drink so much.

h) I would help her if she asked me.

i) If John doesn't improve his English skills, he will fail his exam.

j) If people knew more about this virus, they would be careful.

k) She won't be happy if you tell her the truth.

l) If I was/were a pilot, I would like to fly the Airbus.

m) If I was/were asked, I would like to be a pilot.

n) Your cat will become aggressive if you grap her tail.

o) If you didn't accept this offer, you would be silly.

Who und *what*

1 a) Who did you see at the corner shortly after the accident? Seite 91
b) Whose car came from the right?
c) Who's the driver of the black car?
d) Who has called the police?
e) Whose bike is this?

2 a) Who does she love? Seite 92
b) Who loves her?
c) What does he love?
d) Who did he like?
e) What did you say?
f) Who do you trust?
g) What helped him?
h) Who are you?
i) Who knows you?
j) What is this?
k) Who do you see?
l) Who does she write?

3 a) – Who told you this story? Seite 93
– ~~Who did tell you this story?~~
b) – ~~Who met you in Munich yesterday?~~
– Who did you meet in Munich yesterday?
c) – What did you answer to this silly question?
– ~~What answered you to this silly question?~~
d) – ~~What did the damage cause?~~
– What caused the damage?
e) – ~~Who wrote he so many letters?~~
– Who did he write so many letters?
f) – What did she see?
– ~~What saw she?~~
g) – What do you think?
– ~~What think you?~~
h) – Who protested against the new station building?
– ~~Who did protest against the new station building?~~
i) – ~~Who did say that teachers had to be strict?~~
– Who said that teachers had to be strict?

Fehler-Check

Seite 94

I'm a little zebra and I'm new here at the Blackwood Zoo. So I've got many questions to ask: Who will give me my water? Who's the owner of this zoo? What must I do to get enough food? Who do I have to tell if I feel sick? What do I do after a heavy thunderstorm? Who's this strange man in the white coat? What does "vet" mean? Whose child is this next to the kiosk? What do all the animals do at night? Who will tell me bedtime stories? Who tells me where to get my food in the morning? Who do I have to ask about toys? What do I have for breakfast? Who tells

Lösungen

me about sport activities? Who do I have to go to to ask for new clothes? Who's responsible for lessons in how to annoy lions? What will happen, if I don't go to the zoo school? Whose vehicle can I use when I would like to go on a trip outside the zoo? Who gives me information about holiday camps in Africa?

Relative clauses

Seite 96

1

	notwendig	nicht notwendig
Have you seen the DVD which I bought yesterday?	☒	☐
The book that my sister gave me was boring.	☒	☐
Jill, whose parents are abroad at the moment, likes movies from the 60s.	☐	☒
That's the man who I saw in the bank.	☒	☐
This man, who loves detective stories, is my father.	☐	☒
I don't like the kind of cheese which you brought from the supermarket on Monday.	☒	☐
Mary's shop, which sells second-hand clothes, is open until 4 o'clock in the afternoon.	☐	☒

2
a) Our neighbour, who knows much about butterflies, is out for dinner.
b) ✓
c) Will he meet John, whose daughter's name is Joanne, this afternoon?
d) Mrs Lombard, who likes fast food, won't come to the party.
e) ✓
f) Mr Armstrong, who won the Tour de France several times, lives in the States.
g) ✓
h) ✓
i) The police officer wanted to talk to Mr Wayne, who is a taxi driver.

Seite 97

3
a) This is Jerry, the cat which would like to be mouse.
b) These are the people who tried to catch Jerry.
c) This is the hole which Jerry tried to hide in.
d) This is Sally who rescued Jerry.
e) And this is the milk which poor Jerry is going to drink now.

Seite 98

4
a) The girl ~~which~~/whose/~~that~~ brother is fifteen likes playing tennis.
b) The letter that/~~who~~/which you sent me is two pages long.

c) She doesn't like the kind of music that/~~whose~~/~~who~~/which was played in the circus.

d) Everybody who/~~which~~/that knows how to sail a boat come here, please.

5 a) Our chemistry teacher, ~~that~~/~~which~~/who is 35, will help you with the experiment.

b) Mr Bond gave his son a model airplane, ~~that~~/~~whose~~/which he had bought in the toy shop.

c) Carol Woytyla, who/~~that~~/~~which~~ was a bishop in Poland, became pope.

d) Yesterday I met Sue, ~~that~~/~~which~~/who is always nice to talk to.

Seite 99

6 a) This is the boy Max is afraid of.

b) Where is the book (that/which) I'm looking for?

c) This is the man everybody is proud of.

7 a) John Pearl is the magician who knows how to turn teachers into frogs.

b) The car ~~which~~ we rented in Scotland was brandnew.

c) The man ~~that~~ she was talking to is the chief executive of MM Toys.

d) The company ~~which~~ I work for was founded 10 years ago.

e) Does he know the person that wrote a letter of application to him?

f) Look at the dog which is sitting on the roof!

g) Have you ever met someone who really liked school?

h) Here's the magazine ~~that~~ you wanted to read.

Seite 100

Fehler-Check

London is one of the most beautiful cities -- the world has ever seen. London has got many famous museums and tourist attractions that/which are known all over the world. The Tower Bridge, which is the most famous bridge in London, is visited by millions of tourist every year. The history of London, which is going back to its founding by the Romans, who called it Londinium, is most interesting. London is a city that/which is the world's largest financial centre alongside New York. The Underground, which is the oldest underground railway network in the world, is the second largest in the world after Shanghai. Greater London, which covers an area of 1600 square kilometers, has a population of about 7.5 million. The River Thames is a tidal river that/which makes London vulnerable to flooding. In 1974 people started a project that/which will help to make the city safer – the Thames Barrier. It will hold back water that/which might run into London in periods of heavy rainfall.

L

Lösungen

To-Infinitives – Sätze richtig vereinfachen

Seite 101

1 It's a rainy Sunday morning. Mike doesn't know what to do. It's too boring to sit on the sofa and watch TV. He knows how to play the piano, but he doesn't like to, because he played it for four hours yesterday. Poor Mike. It's absolutely terrible to see him in such a bad mood.

Seite 102

2 a) I don't know how to solve this problem.
b) Did he ask her when to start work?
c) Nice to meet you.
d) It was a big surprise to see my brother.
e) Do you know how to open this file?
f) It was terrible to see the ship sink.
g) It was a good idea to paint this wall.
h) It's a high risk to climb this mountain in winter.
i) Ask him how to help him.

Seite 103

3 a) She didn't know what to answer.
b) I asked him where to go.
c) I was surprised to see Aunt Olivia with her oldtimer car.
d) It was rather difficult to solve the problem so quickly.
e) Can you tell me how to loosen this screw?
f) I told him where to go to get a new passport.

Seite 104

Fehler-Check

9 o'clock. It's difficult to get up so early in the morning. I would prefer to lie/stay in bed all day, but it's not easy to explain this idea to my mother. On the other hand, it's just boring to lie in bed and do nothing. I don't know what to do now. Perhaps it might be a great idea to go to the zoo this Saturday morning, but I don't know how to get there, because the busses aren't running today. They're on strike. It's really terrible to be without a vehicle. My brother's bike is easy to ride, but he's away on a sports camp this weekend. I would like to have/buy my own bike, but it's difficult to get/buy one, if you don't have the money to buy one. I must ask Pete where to get cheap used bikes. Perhaps he knows how to get one. It might be a good plan to go to the sports club today. I would love my mother to take me there, but I think she would prefer to sit/stay in her armchair and read a book. Let's see how I can persuade her to give me a lift. Oh, it's a nuisance to spend a boring Saturday's morning if you don't know what to do!